The
Right Prayers
for
Every Need

Contributing Writers:
Christine A. Dallman
Randy Petersen

Publications International, Ltd.

Christine A. Dallman is a freelance writer who has contributed to the devotional publication, *The Quiet Hour,* and is a former editor and columnist for *Sunday Digest* magazine. She is the author of *Daily Devotions for Seniors,* an inspirational resource for maturing adults, as well as co-author of several other Publications International, Ltd., titles.

Randy Petersen is a writer and church educator from New Jersey with more than 40 books to his credit, including *Red Letters* (Revell) and *Bible Fun Stuff* (Tyndale House). A prolific creator of church curriculum, he's also a contributor to the *Quest Study Bible,* the *Revell Bible Dictionary,* and the iLumina Bible software.

Louis Weber, CEO
Publications International, Ltd.
7373 North Cicero Avenue
Lincolnwood, Illinois 60712

Permission is never granted for commercial purposes.

ISBN-13: 978-1-4127-4545-1
ISBN-10: 1-4127-4545-4

Manufactured in China.

8 7 6 5 4 3 2 1

Library of Congress Control Number: 2009935218

CONTENTS

❊ ❊❊ ❊

TALKING TO GOD

The more we learn about prayer, the more apt we are to turn to God for help, comfort, and guidance. *The Right Prayers for Every Need* is a personal resource that offers representative prayers for a broad spectrum of situations and experiences we encounter in life. In straightforward, everyday language, these prayers echo the thoughts and feelings that rise up from the human heart—from sorrow to gratitude and from loneliness to love.

You may choose to read the book in sequence from cover to cover. Or you can select a chapter title from the table of contents that bests reflects the place in which you find your own heart. In addition, for further reflection on each theme, the prayers are supplemented by compiled and original quotes, as well as Bible verses.

Individual prayers are brief enough to read in a minute or two, providing food for thought throughout the day (or to ponder at bedtime or any other point of quietude in your day). Or you may want to take in an  entire chapter at a time, focusing on the most relevant prayer or prayers for your situation. Part of the beauty of the arrangement of this prayer book is its adaptability to your personal needs.

There are 14 chapters to choose from, and the prayers in each chapter are intended to help draw you into dialogue with an ever-present, approachable God, who lovingly calls you into companionship with himself.

Whether *The Right Prayers for Every Need* becomes a permanent treasure on your personal bookshelf or a gem passed between friends, may you be blessed in some way by the role it plays in supporting and strengthening your growing relationship with the living God.

CHAPTER 1

WHEN YOU'RE
PRAISING
GOD IN
GRATITUDE

✾ ✾ ✾

*Enter his gates with
thanksgiving, and his courts
with praise. Give thanks to him,
bless his name. For the Lord is
good; his steadfast love endures
forever, and his faithfulness
to all generations.*

PSALM 100:4–5

You have turned my mourning
  into dancing;
you have taken off my sackcloth
  and clothed me with joy,
so that my soul may praise you and
  not be silent.
O Lord my God, I will give thanks
  to you forever.

PSALM 30:11–12

Beloved Lord,

You know the struggles I have had lately, but you have brought me through them. Distress has been turned to resilience. Worry has transformed into faith. For a while, I was focusing on my own misfortune, but now you have placed joy in my heart. I feel that I know you better than ever. Thank you for staying beside me in tough times. Lead me forward into better times.

※ ※ ※

The face of grace shows
an attitude of gratitude.

※ ※ ※

Do not worry about anything,
but in everything by prayer and
supplication with thanksgiving let your
requests be made known to God.
And the peace of God, which surpasses
all understanding, will guard your
hearts and your minds.

PHILIPPIANS 4:6–7

※ ※ ※

Everything I have comes from you, dear heavenly Father. I might want a few more zeroes on the right side of my paycheck, and I might sometimes crave a bigger house or a less rusty car, but I am grateful for everything you have provided me. You have given me the ability to work, the ability to love, the ability to worship you, and these are all rich gifts. I praise you for your great kindness to me, now and in the ages to come.

Thanks be to thee, O Lord Jesus Christ,
for all the benefits which thou hast given us;
for all the pains and insults which thou has
borne for us. O most merciful Redeemer,
friend, and brother, may we know
thee more clearly, love thee more dearly,
and follow thee more nearly.

—RICHARD OF CHICHESTER

❋ ❋ ❋

With gratitude in your hearts sing psalms, hymns, and spiritual songs to God. And whatever you do, in word or deed, do everything in the name of the Lord Jesus, giving thanks to God the Father through him.

COLOSSIANS 3:16–17

❋ ❋ ❋

I went to the store today, Lord Jesus, in your name. I talked to a friend today, in your name. I watched TV today, in your name. It's an interesting experiment, doing everything, word or deed, with the awareness that I bear your name. Step by step through my day, I realized that you gave me power to do all that I do. Only through you can I do my daily work, touch the lives of others, and try to make the world a better place. It's your gracious power that keeps me going, and I thank you for that. My gratitude erupts in song. Receive my praises, dear Lord, as the offering of a deeply thankful heart.

❋ ❋ ❋

O Lord that lends me life,
Lend me a heart replete with thankfulness!

—WILLIAM SHAKESPEARE,
HENRY VI, PART II

We give thanks to you, O God;
    we give thanks; your name is near.
People tell of your wondrous deeds.

Psalm 75:1

※ ※ ※

We plow the fields and scatter the
good seed on the land
But it is fed and watered by
God's almighty hand …
All good gifts around us are sent
from heaven above;
Then thank the Lord, O thank
the Lord for all his love.

—Matthias Claudius

Thank you, Creator God, for the amazing wonders of the universe. I watch a sunset, with its rich palette of colors splashing across the sky, and I remember that you made it. Evening turns to night, and the distant stars sparkle against their deep backdrop, each star a sun of another system with planets and moons, and I remember that you made all of that. I reflect on your magnitude, but just when I begin to feel insignificant, I remember that you are near me. Each night you whisper your love. The Creator of all things great and small somehow cares for me in my tiny world. This is even harder to fathom, but I claim it, and I praise you for it.

※ ※ ※

Thanks be to God, who gives us the
victory through our Lord Jesus Christ.
Therefore, my beloved, be steadfast,
immovable, always excelling in the work
of the Lord, because you know that in
the Lord your labor is not in vain.

1 CORINTHIANS 15:57–58

※ ※ ※

A sense of gratitude transforms any situation
from a grudge to a gift.

※ ※ ※

No duty is more urgent than that of
returning thanks.

—AMBROSE

※ ※ ※

Many times in the last year, O Lord, I have felt defeated. The difficulties of daily life nearly overwhelmed me. Money was tight. Relationships were frazzled. My own peace of mind was hanging by a thread. But you, dear Lord, are a winner. You have won the victory over sin and death, and you can win the victory in my life day by day—not necessarily by making everything better (as you know, I still have some struggles), but by reminding me of what's most important and by giving me the confidence to move forward. Life may still be tough, but I know my labor is not meaningless because I'm serving you. Thank you for this new sense of purpose.

※ ※ ※

Riches and honor come from you, and
you rule over all. In your hand are
power and might…. And now, our
God, we give thanks to you and praise
your glorious name.

1 CHRONICLES 29:12–13

※ ※ ※

For years, God, worry has been gnawing at me. No matter how much I talked about trusting you, there was a corner of my mind that always played out the worst scenario. What if. . . ? I imagined all sorts of bad outcomes. But then you wooed me back into faith. I realized that you knew all the contingencies better than I did, and you had them covered. I could bring my worries to you, and you would reshape them into peace. Thank you, Lord, for doing this. Thank you for guarding my heart.

⊗ ⊗ ⊗

Open to me the gates of righteousness,
that I may enter through them
and give thanks to the Lord.

PSALM 118:19

⊗ ⊗ ⊗

Praise isn't just for sports fans, artists, and lovers. It's for all who know they owe their joy to someone else.

Rejoice always, pray without ceasing, give thanks in all circumstances; for this is the will of God in Christ Jesus for you.

1 THESSALONIANS 5:16–18

Almighty God, I humbly bow before you, but you have to admit this is a tall order. Rejoice always? Exactly how am I supposed to pray without ceasing? Do you really want me to give thanks for everything? You know I want to honor you and do your will, but for me to rejoice always, I'd have to believe that you were always doing good things. To give thanks like that, I'd have to think that you were working in every circumstance. To pray without ceasing, I'd have to believe you cared about what I was thinking all the time. That can't really happen, Lord, can it? . . . Oh well, now that I think about it, maybe it can. You'll need to help me, but I'll try.

❈ ❈ ❈

The most important prayer in the world is
just two words long: "Thank you."

—MEISTER ECKHART

Who will rescue me from this body
of death? Thanks be to God through
Jesus Christ our Lord!

ROMANS 7:24–25

※ ※ ※

Dear Savior, it has been a constant struggle
for me to do what's right. You know the
temptations that come my way. Sometimes they
seem overwhelming. My desires are strong.
They pull me away from you. But lately I have
sensed your strength within me. When I have
been tempted, I have turned to you, and you
helped me make a better choice. Thank you, Lord.
Thank you for rescuing me from my sinful desires.

※ ※ ※

Praise, my soul, the King of Heaven,
to the throne thy tribute bring;
Ransomed, healed, restored, forgiven,
evermore God's praises sing.
Alleluia! Alleluia!
Praise the everlasting King!

—HENRY F. LYTE

※ ※ ※

Therefore, since we are receiving a
kingdom that cannot be shaken,
let us give thanks, by which we offer
to God an acceptable worship with
reverence and awe.

HEBREWS 12:28

※ ※ ※

I will praise the name of God
   with a song;
I will magnify him with thanksgiving.

PSALM 69:30

※ ※ ※

Since you're used to the sounds of angel choirs,
my little ditty might not mean that much.
But, Lord, it comes from my heart. You have
done so much for me, I must erupt in a song
of gratitude. Thank you for saving me, for
strengthening me, and for guiding me. Thank
you for the relationships you have provided.
Thank you most of all for the relationship I
have with you. And it's in the tender spirit of
that relationship that I humbly ask you: Enjoy
my song of praise and gratitude.

※ ※ ※

Some have meat they cannot eat
And some want food they lack
But we have meat and we can eat
And so the Lord we thank.

—Adapted from the Selkirk Grace,
attributed to Robert Burns

❋ ❋ ❋

Things change. In my years on earth, heavenly Father, I have learned that well. Just when you think you're holding onto something solid, it moves, it evaporates. Relationships shatter. Jobs get downsized. Fortunes get frittered away. If I put my trust in anything, I am risking disappointment . . . except in you. Your kingdom cannot be shaken. You are the supreme king forever, and I thank you for the mighty role you've played in my life.

❋ ❋ ❋

A thankful heart is not only the greatest virtue,
but the parent of all other virtues.

—CICERO

❈ ❈ ❈

We must always give thanks to God
for you, brothers and sisters, as is
right, because your faith is growing
abundantly, and the love of everyone
of you for one another is increasing.

2 THESSALONIANS 1:3

❈ ❈ ❈

[Let us thank God] for the great degree of
tranquility, union and plenty which
we have enjoyed.

—GEORGE WASHINGTON,
"THANKSGIVING PROCLAMATION"

❈ ❈ ❈

Thank you, Lord, for the wonderful people you have brought into my life. There have been many rich friendships with people who shared my joys and sorrows alike. You have also inspired leaders to teach me and guide me in faith. You have allowed me to have influence on others as well. Thank you, Lord, for this holy community of faith. I don't know what I'd do without them.

※ ※ ※

O give thanks to the Lord,
    for he is good,
for his steadfast love endures forever.

PSALM 136:1

※ ※ ※

Lord, I explode in thanksgiving for your kindness to me. I can't take three steps into the sunshine without feeling gratitude for your creation. The world blossoms with your handiwork—I drink it in with joy. I thank you most deeply for the spiritual blessings you have brought into my life. Though I am a sinner, you have paid my debt and welcomed me into your family. Daily you give me strength to serve you. I am also grateful for the eternal hope you offer me, that my life will not end in this dimension but will go on forever in your heavenly home.

※ ※ ※

Thankfulness is the seed of faith.

※ ※ ※

As you therefore have received
Christ Jesus the Lord, continue to live
your lives in him, rooted and built
up in him and established in the faith,
just as you were taught, abounding
in thanksgiving.

Colossians 2:6–7

✳ ✳ ✳

Lord God Almighty,
I join in that eternal song, giving you thanks
from the very core of my being. You were and
you are. In the past you acted mightily to create,
to call, to redeem, and to win the victory over
death. In the present you reign, you listen, and
you love. I give you thanks today for all that you
are, for all that you have been, and for all the
wonders of the future that I have yet to see.
In Jesus' name, I pray. Amen.

I am grateful to Christ Jesus our Lord, who has strengthened me ... even though I was formerly a blasphemer ... the grace of our Lord overflowed for me with ... faith and love.

1 TIMOTHY 1:12–14

※ ※ ※

Thus might I hide my blushing face
while his dear cross appears;
Dissolve my heart in thankfulness,
and melt mine eyes to tears.
But drops of grief can ne'er repay
the debt of love I owe.
Here, Lord, I give myself away;
'tis all that I can do.

—ISAAC WATTS,
"ALAS AND DID MY SAVIOR BLEED"

※ ※ ※

Nourishing Lord,

I sink my roots deep into your love, and I draw out sustenance. You give me power to live each day, to say no to temptation, and to respond with love to the needs of those around me. Whatever good I do in this world, it's because of you and your great grace. You have built me up. You have helped me grow. Thank you, Lord, for the richness of this life. Thank you for your sustaining love.

※ ※ ※

Then the twenty-four elders...
worshiped God, singing,
"We give you thanks, Lord God
Almighty, who are and who were,
for you have taken your great power
and begun to reign."

REVELATION 11:16–17

※ ※ ※

For the beauty of the earth,
for the glory of the skies,
For the love which from our birth
over and around us lies...
For thyself, best Gift Divine,
to the world so freely given,
for that great, great love of thine,
peace on earth and joy in heaven:
Lord of all, to thee we raise this our hymn
of grateful praise.

—FOLLIOT S. PIERPOINT

God of grace, I can claim no merit of my own.
There is no reason for you to forgive my sin,
other than your great love for me. I have made
bad choices that have hurt others; I'm well aware
of this. But I throw myself on the mercy of your
court, and I find that you are rich in mercy.
You forgive my sin, you heal my heart, and you
bring me into an exciting kinship with you.
This is not my doing, it's yours, and I thank you
for it. My heart overflows with gratitude for your
grace and mercy. I will tell everyone I know about
what you have done for me. My life now has
a soundtrack, a song of thanksgiving.

※ ※ ※

All praise and thanks to
God the Father now be given;
The Son, and him who reigns
with them in highest heaven;
The one eternal God,
whom earth and heaven adore;
For thus it was, is now,
and shall be evermore.

—Martin Rinkart,
"Now Thank We All Our God"

CHAPTER 2

WHEN YOU'RE
SEEKING
GUIDANCE

※ ※ ※

By the tender mercy of our God,
the dawn from on high will
break upon us, to give light to
those who sit in darkness and in
the shadow of death, to guide
our feet into the way of peace.

LUKE 1:78–79

※ ※ ※

The Lord is my shepherd,
I shall not want.
He makes me lie down in
green pastures;
he leads me beside still waters;
he restores my soul.
He leads me in right paths
for his name's sake.

PSALM 23:1–3

Dear Lord,
I need you to shepherd me through my life.
I know how easily I can go astray, and I know
I need your rod and staff to keep me headed in
the right direction. I don't even know what the
right direction is, but I trust you to lead me.
Green pastures, still waters—I am grateful for
the blissful moments you provide, but most of all
I thank you for your presence beside me, helping
me find my way. With your guidance, I will live
each day "for your name's sake."

❈ ❈ ❈

If the Lord is our shepherd, that makes us
sheep, prone to wander and bleat a lot.

❈ ❈ ❈

When the Spirit of truth comes,
he will guide you into all the truth;
for he will not speak on his own,
but will speak whatever he hears,
and he will declare to you the things
that are to come.

John 16:13

❋ ❋ ❋

Trust in the Lord with all your heart,
    and do not rely on your own insight.
In all your ways acknowledge him,
    and he will make straight your paths.

Proverbs 3:5–6

❋ ❋ ❋

Triune God—Father, Son, and Holy Spirit—
I ask you to keep speaking truth to me. Sometimes I don't want to hear it. I want to go my
willful way, and I know you'll just delay me.
Then there are other times when your voice gets
drowned out by the other sounds around me.
It seems there's always a TV blaring, a computer
humming, a cell phone ringing, an alarm
beeping, and people complaining. That can
make it hard to hear you. But now I'll focus my
spiritual ears on that "still, small voice" of yours.
I'll listen for your gentle whisper. Keep sending
your message of truth in my direction, and I'll
pay attention, because ultimately yours is the
only voice that makes sense.

Spirit of God, descend upon my heart;
Wean it from earth; through all its pulses move;
Stoop to my weakness, mighty as thou art,
And make me love thee as I ought to love.

—GEORGE CROLY,
"SPIRIT OF GOD, DESCEND UPON MY HEART"

※ ※ ※

It must be admitted that a life is properly formed
when and only when it is yielded to God.

—JOHN CALVIN

※ ※ ※

Walk about Zion, go all around it,
    count its towers...,
that you may tell the next generation
    that this is God,
our God forever and ever.
    He will be our guide forever.

PSALM 48:12–14

*Too often, my Lord, I make my own plans and
forget about yours. I think I know what's best
for me, and I set out my goals accordingly.
But now I see that this isn't just ungodly,
it's not smart. What do I know, compared to
you? Do I really expect that I can make wise
decisions independent of you? My Creator,
you made me! You know how I function best!
Besides that, you know the rest of the world as
well, and what effect I can have on it. So, Lord,
right here and now, I acknowledge you. Be my
guide through life. Make my paths straight.*

❈ ❈ ❈

The best gift for the young is giving them
a relationship with God.

❈ ❈ ❈

Whatever I have built in my life, O God,
it's because of you. Whatever home I have,
whatever career I've established, whatever
fortune I've amassed, whatever relationships
I treasure—it's all because you have guided me.
I owe it all to you. Thank you for these things,
and please give me opportunities to tell the next
generation of your love and power.

※ ※ ※

May [God] give you a spirit of wisdom
and revelation as you come to know
him, so that, with the eyes of your
heart enlightened, you may know what
is the hope to which he has called you.

EPHESIANS 1:17–18

※ ※ ※

Lord of light, shine your presence deep into my life. Enlighten my heart, and show me the way you want me to go. As I weigh my options, I try to figure out where each path will lead, but it's hard for me to see clearly. Give me your wisdom. Help me understand what's most important to you. Let me see through the guises of deceivers, and let me enjoy the beautiful visage of truth. I want your Spirit to radiate through me and outward to others. Let me shine for you.

❈ ❈ ❈

Remember the little girl who closed her eyes so she couldn't see you while playing hide-and-seek? We do something similar with God: We close our eyes and think he's hiding from us. Want to find him? Open the eyes of your heart.

❈ ❈ ❈

I am continually with you;
   you hold my right hand.
You guide me with your counsel…
Whom have I in heaven but you?
And there is nothing on earth that
   I desire other than you.

PSALM 73:23–25

※ ※ ※

Dear heavenly Father,
You gave birth to my soul, and I think of you
now as a parent guiding my first steps. My
hands are held firmly in yours as I venture
forward. Will I move safely across the room, or
will I fall flat? I'm not afraid of falling because
you are holding me, step by step by step. I'm older
now, and I've been walking on my own for years
now, and yet I still hold on to you in a spiritual
sense. I rely on your guidance to know that I'm
doing the right thing. I know I need your counsel.
Especially now, my God, especially now I need
to hold your hand. I need your guidance more
than ever.

※ ※ ※

Guide me, O thou great Jehovah,

pilgrim through this barren land.

I am weak, but thou art mighty;

hold me with thy powerful hand.

Bread of heaven, bread of heaven,

feed me till I want no more,

Feed me till I want no more.

—William Williams,
"Guide Me, O Thou Great Jehovah"

※ ※ ※

I will lead the blind

by a road they do not know,

by paths they have not known

I will guide them.

I will turn the darkness before them

into light,

the rough places into level ground.

Isaiah 42:16

I feel as if I'm blind right now, my Lord. I feel
as if I'm in total darkness. This is uncharted
territory for me. I can imagine this road leading
to great success or dismal failure. I don't know
what to do. So please, Lord, I beg you, guide
me through this rough terrain. Let me see where
you want me to go. I want to be obedient to
your will.

❈ ❈ ❈

O! for a closer walk with God,
A calm and heav'nly frame;
A light to shine upon the road
That leads me to the Lamb!

—WILLIAM COWPER,
"WALKING WITH GOD"

❈ ❈ ❈

We have not ceased praying for you
and asking that you may be filled with
the knowledge of God's will in all
spiritual wisdom and understanding,
so that you may lead lives worthy of
the Lord, fully pleasing to him.

Colossians 1:9–10

❈ ❈ ❈

God of all wisdom, I need some wisdom today.
Decisions need to be made, and I'm clueless.
I want to do not only the right thing but also
the good thing. I want to honor you, to affect
others in positive ways, and to make a difference
in the world. But how? The choices before me are
equally confusing. Can you show me the right
and wrong here, the good and the better?
Share that insight with me, please!

❈ ❈ ❈

The wise want love,
and those who love want wisdom.

—PERCY BYSSHE SHELLEY,
"PROMETHEUS UNBOUND"

※ ※ ※

Bind [your parents' teachings] upon
your heart always;
tie them around your neck.
When you walk, they will lead you;
when you lie down, they will watch
over you;
and when you awake, they will talk
with you.

PROVERBS 6:21–22

❋ ❋ ❋

Dear Lord,

I thank you for those who have taught me about you. They planted a seed in my heart that still grows. I thank you for the traditions they gave me and for all the faithful ones who have passed down those traditions through the centuries. I am deeply grateful. But now I need to draw from that vast reservoir. Life has become confusing. I need to know what to do and where to go. So speak to me now through your Word. Guide me in my day-to-day decisions. Summon up old recollections of Bible stories and memory verses, and let them lead me through the days ahead. Bring your words to my mind as I need them. And I will continue to thank you.

❋ ❋ ❋

We work hard to "rightly divide the Word of truth," but if God's Word is like a "two-edged sword," then it needs to "rightly divide" us.

Almighty God, I'm asking for wisdom, your wisdom. Help me make some good decisions at this juncture of my life. Whenever I follow my own desires, I make a mess of things. You keep challenging me to hold off and take a look at my priorities—and at your priorities—before I move forward. I know I should listen to you more. So now I'm listening. Please give me some of the wisdom I so desperately need.

❊ ❊ ❊

Some tell us that we must earn spiritual
blessings. But Jesus says, "Just ask."

❈ ❈ ❈

If any of you is lacking in wisdom, ask God,
who gives to all generously and ungrudgingly,
and it will be given you.

JAMES 1:5

❈ ❈ ❈

They shall not hunger or thirst,
  neither scorching wind nor sun shall
    strike them down,
for he who has pity on them will lead
  them,
    and by springs of water will guide
      them.

ISAIAH 49:10

※ ※ ※

All the way my Savior leads me,
  cheers each winding path I tread
Gives me grace for every trial,
  feeds me with the living bread.
Though my weary steps may falter,
  and my soul athirst may be,
Gushing from the rock before me, lo!
  A spring of joy I see.

—FANNY CROSBY,
"ALL THE WAY MY SAVIOR LEADS ME"

O Lord, sometimes it seems that I'm traveling
through a vast desert. I trudge through
the shifting sands with little idea of where
I'm going, and refreshment is hard to come by.
But then I look to you, and I remember your
promises. You promise to provide for me,
quenching my spiritual hunger and thirst.
And you say you'll guide me, giving me direction
and motivation. Thank you for showing pity
on me in my desperate, aimless times, and I
trust you to lead me safely through all the arid
places of my life.

❋ ❋ ❋

Teach me to do your will,
for you are my God.
Let your good spirit lead me
on a level path.

PSALM 143:10

O my Savior, teach me. I've spent far too long assuming that I knew everything I needed to know, but now I realize I don't. I need to become your pupil, to sit at your feet, and to learn. How do you want me to live? What makes you happy? How can I live a truly abundant life, with joy overflowing to others? How can I develop good relationships, with your kind of love replacing my kind of selfishness? And considering that you made me, it makes sense to ask you how I can live most effectively, doing the things you originally intended. I want to learn these things, and I'm sure there's more that I don't even know. Teach me, Lord; I'm listening.

Accept the accidents that occur
to you as good, since you know that nothing
occurs apart from God.

—DIDACHE

⁂ ⁂ ⁂

The Lamb at the center of the throne
will be their shepherd,
and he will guide them to springs of
the water of life,
and God will wipe away every tear
from their eyes.

REVELATION 7:17

⁂ ⁂ ⁂

For the believer,
eternal life has already started.

⁂ ⁂ ⁂

O Lamb of God, I look forward to the day when I worship you in the carefree bliss of heaven, when I drink the water of life from ever-flowing springs, and when all the woes of this world get wiped away. What a day that will be! But now I still struggle, and I ask you to shepherd me. Help me live the life you have prepared for me, overcoming the obstacles of this world on a steady journey from today to eternity.

※ ※ ※

The wisdom from above is first pure,
then peaceable, gentle, willing to yield,
full of mercy and good fruits, without
a trace of partiality or hypocrisy.

JAMES 3:17

※ ※ ※

I've had enough of worldly wisdom, dear Lord, from so-called sages who tell me that money buys happiness or success brings friends. They say I should put myself first, indulging my desires and ignoring others. This, I'm told, is the path to fulfillment. But that can't be right, can it? Lord, I ask for an extra helping of your "wisdom from above." Show me how to treat others with gentle love. Teach me to deal peaceably with the challenges in my life. Help me be fruitful and merciful. Erase the petty prejudice that keeps me from appreciating your other children. Let me yield fully to your perfect wisdom and set aside the tame truisms of this world.

※ ※ ※

God not only orders our steps.
He orders our stops.

—George Muller

My dear Lord,
There are days when I feel weak in body and
spirit. I count on you for strength. There are
days when I feel empty. I trust you to satisfy
me. Some days I feel dry, devoid of life and
hope. Please, O Lord, sprinkle your living water
over every aspect of my life. Other times I need
direction, and I humbly ask you: Guide me,
precious Lord.

※ ※ ※

The woman at the well offered
Jesus a drink of water,
and he promised her living water.
Isn't that how it goes? He enjoys our gifts,
but he returns something far better.

※ ※ ※

I am thoroughly sinful myself, and I have not
yet eluded temptation, but I'm stuck in the
middle of the devil's devices—still I strive to
follow righteousness.

—SECOND EPISTLE OF CLEMENT

※ ※ ※

Dear Jesus,
I want to keep my priorities straight, but it isn't
easy. I want you to rule over my life, but I keep
taking that throne for myself. I want your
righteousness to flow through everything I do,
but I struggle daily with temptation. I want to
trust you for the daily stuff of life, but all too
often I begin to fret about those things. But
today I commit myself anew. Let me strive first
for your kingdom, dear Lord, and trust you for
everything else. In your name, I pray. Amen.

※ ※ ※

CHAPTER 3

WHEN YOU'RE FACING FEAR OR DANGER

✳ ✳ ✳

Those who love me,
I will deliver; I will protect those
who know my name.
When they call to me,
I will answer them;
I will be with them in trouble,
I will rescue them and
honor them.

PSALM 91:14–15

Be strong and courageous; do not
be frightened or dismayed, for the
Lord your God is with you wherever
you go.

JOSHUA 1:9

✵ ✵ ✵

*Thank you, Lord, that you're never missing
in action—that you're with me all the time,
everywhere, without fail. Please keep this
knowledge in the forefront of my mind today
so I'll be encouraged and emboldened to
move through each challenge without feeling
intimidated, fearful, or ashamed. May I
always be kept safe because you are at work
in my life. In your name, I pray. Amen.*

✵ ✵ ✵

I lie down and sleep;
  I wake again, for the Lord
    sustains me.
I am not afraid of ten thousands
    of people
  who have set themselves against
    me all around.

PSALM 3:5–6

❋ ❋ ❋

As I face the "big stuff" right now, Lord, help me remember that the magnitude of the danger does not affect or change your ability to protect me. Because you're all-powerful, there is nothing too big or too small for you. I know that is true, whether I have one foe or a million. When I choose to follow you, I'm on the winning team. Please help me keep my eyes on how great you are instead of how big the danger or the challenge is so that my faith in you won't waver or dissolve. And I ask that my sleep will be sweet tonight as I commit myself to your care of me.

※ ※ ※

When you stand at God's side, you can be sure you're standing on the side of victory.

※ ※ ※

The Lord is my light and my salvation;
whom shall I fear? The Lord is the
stronghold of my life; of whom shall I
be afraid? . . . Though an army encamp
against me, my heart shall not fear.

PSALM 27:1, 3

❋ ❋ ❋

The best way to see divine light is
to put out thine own candle.

—THOMAS FULLER,
GNOMOLOGIA

❋ ❋ ❋

When I am afraid, I put my trust in you.
In God, whose word I praise,
in God I trust; I am not afraid;
what can flesh do to me?

PSALM 56:3–4

❋ ❋ ❋

Sometimes, Lord, I find myself staring into the darkness "out there" and feeling defeated by the vastness of it, afraid I'll be overwhelmed or overtaken by it. It seems the darkness is all around me; it is even in the lives of some of the people I love most. There are days when I'm frightened, when I feel as if I'm the only one with a faith-filled perspective. Some people think I'm naïve or foolish or out of touch when I say I trust in you. But I know you are the one who has saved me and kept me and who will continue to do so. Help me not "cave in" to the pressure of the darkness of cynicism and fear. Let your presence shine all the brighter through me today as you fill me with the light of a renewed faith.

※ ※ ※

To open our heart and mind to trust
God's Word is to slam shut
the doors of fear.

*Your Word is like a powerful stream of water
that washes the doubt and fear from my
mind and refreshes my faith and confidence
in you. Remind me to keep the stream flowing
by opening the Scriptures regularly and
reading them, whether or not I am feeling
very "devotional" or "spiritual." As I am less
fearful and walk in faith more, let your Word
be the catalyst you intend it to be in setting me
free from my fear.*

For the righteous will never be moved;
they will be remembered forever.
They are not afraid of evil tidings;
their hearts are firm, secure in the Lord.

PSALM 112:6–7

※ ※ ※

If I react to bad news in fear or panic, dear Lord, it just adds to the problem. Of course, even though I know this, sometimes what I hear just takes me by surprise. So please help me look to you when bad tidings come. Help me be still as you show me how to respond in faith. May faith win the day right now as I stand my ground, trusting in you against any danger.

※ ※ ※

Bad news doesn't *change* who God is; rather, it challenges us to *trust* who he is.

❈ ❈ ❈

Do not be afraid of sudden panic,
or of the storm that strikes the wicked;
for the Lord will be your confidence and
will keep your foot from being caught.

PROVERBS 3:25–26

❈ ❈ ❈

Heavenly Father,
There is so much crazy stuff going on in the
world! There are people saying, "It's the end."
There is global warming, the threat of terrorism,
the instability of the world's economy, corruption
and crime, and all sorts of other disturbing
news. It seems as if evil in the world is increasing
everywhere, and there are times I'm afraid
of what's going to happen next. But I know
you keep your children in your care. Help me
not be afraid. Help me seek you as the refuge
not only for my physical well-being but also
for the peace of mind that I need in a world
that will never be capable of offering me any
guarantees. You are my one and only guarantee,
and you guarantee everything I need in this life
and beyond.

※ ※ ※

Trusting God in the chaos is
like standing in the eye of a hurricane.
There is no safe place outside of that trust and
nothing but safety inside of it.

⁕ ⁕ ⁕

The angel said to the women, "Do not
be afraid; I know that you are looking
for Jesus who was crucified. He is not
here; for he has been raised, as he said.
Come, see the place where he lay."

MATTHEW 28:5–6

⁕ ⁕ ⁕

Because Jesus keeps his promise of peace,
his promise of peace will keep us safe.

⁕ ⁕ ⁕

Dear Jesus,

It is the power of your resurrection that reminds me that there's no reason for me to fear the worst, not even death. My trust is in a risen Savior, over whom death has no power. I don't need any other evidence to convince me that you are equal to whatever may seem to threaten my life or the lives of the ones I love. What a powerful confidence you've provided for me in your victory over the grave! I offer you my praise today.

※ ※ ※

It is when our fears finally die that we know
a true faith has risen to life.

※ ※ ※

[Jesus said,] "Peace I leave with you;
my peace I give to you. I do not give
to you as the world gives. Do not let
your hearts be troubled, and do not let
them be afraid."

JOHN 14:27

❈ ❈ ❈

*The inner peace you provide, Almighty Lord,
is unruffled and fearless, resting on a firm
foundation of faith in you. It's a gift you left to
your followers—including me—for all time.
I have learned that it's not like the circumstantial
peace the world offers, based on conditions of
health and wealth and situation. Your peace is
rock solid in every circumstance, good or bad.
Please hold me in that gift of peace today
and always.*

❈ ❈ ❈

He who dwells in the shelter of the
Most High will rest in the shadow of
the Almighty. I will say of the Lord,
"He is my refuge and my fortress,
my God, in whom I trust."

PSALM 91:1–2 (NIV)

※ ※ ※

*Today, dear Lord, as an act of faith, I declare
my trust in you out loud! I say, "The Lord is my
refuge, my fortress, the God in whom I place my
trust!" I will say it as I get ready to greet the day,
as I move from place to place, as I take my meals,
and when I lie down to rest. Let each declaration
seal the truth to my heart and mind. Thank you
for being my shelter and safe place during this
storm of life. I'll say it again, "You are my God,
in whom I trust." Amen!*

※ ※ ※

Faith speaks, acts, and behaves with patient confidence in God's power, anticipating his goodness as his plan unfolds.

※ ※ ※

Strengthen the weak hands, and make firm the feeble knees. Say to those who are of a fearful heart, "Be strong, do not fear! Here is your God.... He will come and save you."

ISAIAH 35:3–4

Two of the best things we can do to encourage others are simply to pray for them and to point them toward God's love.

※ ※ ※

Lord, I've noticed that as I encourage myself in you, those around me are encouraged as well. It can feel like a big responsibility, though, to be the one who is "rallying the troops." To be honest, sometimes I feel weak and afraid and as if I'm not up to being "the strong one." O, how I need to lean into you and remember that you are the strong one, not me! You are the source of my strength and courage, and it's only as I stay close to you that I am made strong. Let my trust in you sustain me today and point others to trust in you as well.

❈ ❈ ❈

A prudent man sees danger and takes refuge, but the simple keep going and suffer for it.

PROVERBS 22:3 (NIV)

❈ ❈ ❈

Wisdom and common sense in the context
of faith in God are powerful allies in
a dangerous world.

❖ ❖ ❖

Who shall separate us from the love
of Christ? Shall trouble or hardship or
persecution or famine or nakedness or
danger or sword? . . . No, in all these
things we are more than conquerors
through him who loved us.

ROMANS 8:35, 37 (NIV)

※ ※ ※

Lord Jesus,

When I feel separated from you, I feel insecure, vulnerable, and unsafe. Sometimes I feel separated from you when I'm flailing around in the "soup of life" and haven't touched base with you for quite a while. But your Word promises that nothing in this world can truly separate me from you. My life is yours, and in you, each uncertain circumstance is an opportunity to experience a victory through you. Thank you for your unfailing love and support through it all. Let this time of connection with you right now cause me to be reassured of these things. In your name, I pray. Amen.

※ ※ ※

Adverse circumstances are the laboratories of life in which our faith is purified, refined, proven, and grown.

I am convinced that neither death
nor life, . . . neither the present nor
the future . . . nor anything else in all
creation, will be able to separate us
from the love of God that is in Christ
Jesus our Lord.

Romans 8:38–39 (NIV)

❈ ❈ ❈

Dear heavenly Father,
I want to remember the scope of your protective
love, which covers anything and everything I may
face in life, including what's before me right now.
Please hold me in your love today—safe, secure,
and comforted. Let your love chase away the
cares and fears and worries that I carry as it
protects me—heart, soul, mind, and body.

❈ ❈ ❈

The surest things in life are not death and taxes
but the existence of God and the reality of
his unfailing love for us.

❋ ❋ ❋

The disciples went and woke [Jesus],
saying, "Lord, save us! We're going to
drown!" He replied, "You of little faith,
why are you so afraid?" Then he got up
and rebuked the winds and the waves,
and it was completely calm.

MATTHEW 8:25–26 (NIV)

❋ ❋ ❋

Little faith panics; growing faith prays;
seasoned faith walks on water in
the middle of the storm.

❋ ❋ ❋

Dear Jesus,

When I remember who you are, my fear soon subsides (like that wind and those waves), and my heart becomes completely calm. Speak peace to my soul right now, I pray, and remind me that I am not going to drown in the sea of life as long as you are with me. Grow my little faith into a big faith that can trust you, unshaken, in any and all dangers.

※ ※ ※

Are not two sparrows sold for a penny?
Yet not one of them will fall to the
ground apart from your Father....
So do not be afraid; you are of more
value than many sparrows.

MATTHEW 10:29, 31

※ ※ ※

*Your Word says you know how many hairs
are on my head right now; you are that
attentive to the details of my life. Why, then,
do I sometimes think you're not aware of
my circumstances? Heavenly Father, your love
for me is thorough and painstaking. I'm sorry
for the times I've accused you of not caring.
You are always inviting me to bring my cares to
you because you do care for me. What a wonderful
invitation! The God who created the universe
has made me his own child and invites me to
come to him for everything I need. I must pour
all of these fears and anxieties from my heart
into your capable hands. May my fear evaporate
completely as I come to you right now.*

※ ※ ※

Fear is like a specter that follows us around, whispering messages of impending dread and doom. Faith is like a shield that goes before us, leading us in songs of inevitable joy and victory.

✳ ✳ ✳

My help comes from the Lord,
who made heaven and earth....
He who keeps you will not slumber....
The Lord will keep your going out
and your coming in from this time
on and forevermore.

Psalm 121:2–3, 8

✳ ✳ ✳

What a relief to know that God is never "off duty," that it's perfectly fine for us to take a permanent break from our fears and worries!

✳ ✳ ✳

In a crisis, when I call my best friend to help calm me down, when I indulge in comfort foods to ease my anxiety, when I exercise or take a drive to escape in an effort to lower my blood pressure, Lord, thank you for these temporary measures of relief. But I know that my true help comes only from you. My friends have to sleep, but you don't. My food runs out and upsets my stomach, but you satisfy me with a lasting comfort and peace. The benefits of exercise and temporary escapes fade away, but your love is eternal. I look to you, Lord, when I am afraid or in danger. I call on you. I trust in you, now and forever. Be my true helper, my keeper, and my rescuer. In Jesus' name, I pray. Amen.

CHAPTER 4

WHEN YOU'RE
FEELING
FRUSTRATED
OR
OVERWHELMED

Hear my cry, O God;
Attend unto my prayer....
When my heart is overwhelmed;
Lead me to the rock that is
higher than I.

PSALM 61:1–2 (NKJV)

Give ear to my prayer, O God; and
hide not thyself from my supplication!
Attend to me, and answer me;
I am overcome by my trouble.
I am distraught.

PSALM 55:1–2 (RSV)

❈ ❈ ❈

The worst things:
To be in bed and sleep not,
To want for one who comes not,
To try to please and please not.

—EGYPTIAN PROVERB

❈ ❈ ❈

O God!

I'm so frustrated. I feel as if every time I turn around, another thing breaks or goes wrong or has to be done, and it's all up to me. My nerves and emotions are stretched to the limit. My mind won't quiet down at night, so I don't get the rest I need. Even my dreams are full of futile attempts to get something accomplished. Help me! Please! I can't seem to quiet myself, and I just can't take one more task or problem. I need to be in your presence where you can quiet me with your love. So here I am. Please look for me. I desperately need you right now.

❋ ❋ ❋

It is in vain that you rise up early
and go late to rest, eating the bread
of anxious toil; for he gives sleep
to his beloved.

PSALM 127:2

Heavenly Father,
Please show me how to be at rest in body,
mind, and spirit as I go through this long day.
My stressed-out mode is an exercise in futility
and robs me not only of efficiency but also of
enjoyment. Help me trust you enough to do only
what I can reasonably do, leaving everything else
for another day. Help me open my mind to
your redirection, whether it means canceling,
rescheduling, or even letting go of what you
don't have planned for me today. Here I am once
again. Grant me a restful soul in the daytime and
a peaceful sleep at night, for your name's sake.
Amen.

❧ ❧ ❧

Anxiety weighs down the human heart,
but a good word cheers it up.

PROVERBS 12:25

Sleep that knits up the ravelled sleeve of care,
The death of each day's life, sore labour's bath,
Balm of hurt minds, great nature's
second course,
Chief nourisher in life's feast.

—SHAKESPEARE, *MACBETH*

❋ ❋ ❋

How I need to hear a good word from you right now, precious Lord! Please encourage and soothe my overwrought heart with the Scriptures by the voice of your Spirit. There is nothing else like the comfort and peace that comes when you speak to me. I ask, too, that you would cause your words to echo in my mind all day long, no matter what the day brings.

❋ ❋ ❋

Blessed quietness, holy quietness,
What assurance in my soul!
On the stormy sea He speaks peace to me.
How the billows cease to roll!

—MANIE P. FERGUSON,
"BLESSED QUIETNESS"

※ ※ ※

Therefore I tell you, do not worry
about your life, what you will eat or
what you will drink, or about your
body, what you will wear. Is not life
more than food, and the body more
than clothing?

MATTHEW 6:25

I just don't see how I'm going to make ends meet this time, O Lord! There aren't enough resources to stretch over all these needs and obligations. I'm fighting panic and despair. Please help me trust you as my provider, and help me resist, I pray, the temptation to dictate to you how and when the providing should be done. Remind me of other times you have brought what I needed, and as I focus on your faithfulness, put a song of thanksgiving in my heart for the way you've taken care of me up till now. The reality is that I'm not living in a cardboard box. I'm not eating dandelion soup. I'm not naked. You are here with me, and you are taking care of me. Let that reality sink in and stay with me today. In Jesus' most precious name, I pray. Amen.

※ ※ ※

The virtue of prosperity is temperance;
the virtue of adversity is fortitude.

—Francis Bacon,
"Of Adversity," *Essays*

※ ※ ※

So do not worry about tomorrow,
for tomorrow will bring worries
of its own. Today's trouble is enough
for today.

Matthew 6:34

※ ※ ※

Do not be anxious about anything, but
in everything, by prayer and petition,
with thanksgiving, present your
requests to God. And the peace of
God…will guard your hearts and your
minds in Christ Jesus.

Philippians 4:6–7 (niv)

Dear Lord,

What is the world coming to? Every time I read the newspaper, every time I turn on the radio or television, there are reports that stir up insecurity in me about the future. What is going to happen with the economy, this society, our government, the earth itself? What will my life look like in ten years? What will the next generation be facing? How are my grandchildren going to fare in this world? It feels as though everything is falling apart.

But I know the future is in your hands, Lord. So help me be faithful to what you have for me to do today and to let you take care of what lies ahead. Remind me that you have a plan and that I can trust you.

❋ ❋ ❋

I never think of the future.
It comes soon enough.

—ALBERT EINSTEIN

※ ※ ※

Heavenly Father,
I have this false notion that worry is my personal
duty—that I've not given proper consideration
to that worry until I've fretted about it for a
time. I know that's foolish thinking, Lord, but
I do this without thinking, and therein lies my
constant problem. Please bring it to my attention
when I need to pray, before I start to worry. Let
prayer become my first response in any situation
so that my worries don't overwhelm me. In Jesus'
name, I pray. Amen.

※ ※ ※

Of course, the temptation is to worry first
and pray later, but it is more efficient
to pray first, rendering the step
of worry unnecessary.

※ ※ ※

Be still before the Lord, and wait
patiently for him; do not fret over
those who…carry out evil devices.
Do not fret—it leads only to evil.

PSALM 37:7–8

※ ※ ※

It's hard not to get frustrated and worked up about the people in my life who go out of their way to harm me, Lord. It's especially hard when I've done my best to make peace, to keep peace, to turn the other cheek, to do all the things I know are right and good. Please intervene for me. I'm tired of the alternating hurt and anger that comes when I dwell on the injustices. Help me not fret but just trust that you see and know.

✵ ✵ ✵

Neither evil tongues,
Rash judgements, nor the sneers of selfish men,
Nor greetings where no kindness is, nor all
The dreary intercourse of daily life,
Shall e'er prevail against us.

—WILLIAM WORDSWORTH,
"LINES WRITTEN A FEW MILES ABOVE TINTERN ABBEY"

✵ ✵ ✵

May you be strengthened with all
power, according to his glorious might,
for all endurance and patience with joy.

COLOSSIANS 1:11 (RSV)

※ ※ ※

Almighty Father,
It's been said that life is a marathon, not a sprint,
and your Word tells us to run the race that is
before us with endurance. But I feel right now
as if I'm at the point in the marathon where
I've "hit the wall" and can't go on. I'm out of
strength and energy. I'm really worn out and
overwhelmed with exhaustion. How grateful
I am that I can come to you today! You are all
powerful; your strength is inexhaustible. In you
I know I can find what I need to endure, and not
only to endure but also to run with joy.

※ ※ ※

He giveth more grace when
the burdens grow greater;
He sendeth more strength when
the labors increase;
To added affliction, He addeth His mercy;
To multiplied trials, His multiplied peace.

—ANNIE J. FLINT,
"HE GIVETH MORE GRACE"

※ ※ ※

If I say, "Surely the darkness will
overwhelm me,
And the light around me will be night,"
Even the darkness is not dark to You,
And the night is as bright as the day.
Darkness and light are alike to You.

PSALM 139:11–12 (NASB)

※ ※ ※

I feel as if I'm lost deep in a dark cave, Lord Jesus. I don't know where to put my foot next. I'm afraid to move. I'm afraid to stand still. I'm afraid I'll never find my way out of this darkness. O God who sees the beginning from the end, for whom darkness is as light, please take hold of my hand and lead me to safety and peace. Help me trust you as you lead, and help me stay with you, even when my fear is gone.

※ ※ ※

The reality of darkness ultimately serves to make evident the glory of God's light.

※ ※ ※

Cast all your anxiety on him,
because he cares for you.

1 PETER 5:7

※ ※ ※

I'm here, my Lord, with a full load of frustrations and anxieties. More than I can carry. All I can say is thank you that you care, that I can cast them away as I pray, leaving them with you. Help me, Lord, not take them back today. Remind me to leave them with you, where they belong.

※ ※ ※

As we learn to lean into God,
we learn what it means that he *is* God.

※ ※ ※

When my spirit was overwhelmed
within me, You knew my path.

PSALM 142:3 (NASB)

❋ ❋ ❋

*I feel like sitting down never to rise up again,
Lord. I'm tired and confused. I've come this
far, and I don't even know how I got here. And
I certainly don't know where to go from here.
Whether it's a dead end, a narrow path, or a
superhighway I'm on, I really don't know, and
to be honest, I hardly care. And yet, I know that
giving up isn't an option, dear Lord. I know that
I must give up full control to you—that's what
I need to do. You know my path—where I've
come from, where I've come to, and where I need
to go. I'm ready to follow you away from here
and into the plans you have for me.*

❋ ❋ ❋

It may be in the valley where
countless dangers hide;
It may be in the sunshine that I in peace abide
But this one thing I know—if it be dark or fair,
If Jesus is with me, I'll go anywhere.

—C. Austin Miles,
"If Jesus Goes with Me"

※ ※ ※

Teach me to do Your will,
For You are my God;
Your Spirit is good....
Revive me, O Lord, for Your
name's sake!
For Your righteousness' sake bring
my soul out of trouble.

Psalm 143:10–11 (NKJV)

※ ※ ※

I believe that there are lessons for me to carry out of this place of frustration and that there is good you can bring forth from this troubled soul of mine, Lord. Please grant me a willing spirit to learn what you are teaching me. And, Lord, please don't let your refreshment and restoration be too far off.

※ ※ ※

God's mercies are like rains that fall from heaven on our souls. If we weren't thirsty for them from time to time, we would likely neither recognize nor appreciate them.

※ ※ ※

Blessed is the man who trusts in the
Lord.... He will be like a tree planted
by the water.... It does not fear when
heat comes; its leaves are always green.

JEREMIAH 17:7–8 (NIV)

❊ ❊ ❊

*I can see how these circumstances are pressing
me to press into you, dear Lord. I can see
growth in my perspective about trusting you.
And even though my situation is the same,
I'm not the same. I'm learning how to be calm in
the chaos; strong in the struggle; peaceful in the
pressure. Frustration comes, but doesn't stay;
my heart is overwhelmed, but then it overcomes.
It's all because I've learned to keep my soul
tapped into you, dear Lord. Thank you for
these lessons; thank you for this growth.*

❊ ❊ ❊

Strangely enough, the greatest spiritual
growth can happen in the most adverse
circumstances—and it often does.

❋ ❋ ❋

Who of you by worrying can add
a single hour to his life?

MATTHEW 6:27 (NIV)

❋ ❋ ❋

Worry warts are unsightly lumps on our souls,
growing ever bigger if left untreated with
adequate applications of faith.

❋ ❋ ❋

Rejoice in your hope,
be patient in tribulation,
be constant in prayer.

ROMANS 12:12 (RSV)

Remind me again today, O God, of the futility of fretting. Can I list one accomplishment from allowing worry into my heart? Not one. Today, by your grace, I resolve that even when I feel circumstances have completely overwhelmed me, I will not waste precious time by being anxious and stressed out. Instead, I'll spend that time talking with you, inviting you into my circumstances so that your will can be accomplished in them.

※ ※ ※

Turn your eyes upon Jesus,
Look full in His wonderful face;
And the things of earth will grow strangely dim
In the light of His glory and grace.

—HELEN H. LEMMEL,
"TURN YOUR EYES UPON JESUS"

※ ※ ※

So be truly glad. There is wonderful
joy ahead, even though you have to
endure many trials for a little while.
These trials will show that your faith
is genuine. It is being tested as fire tests
and purifies gold.

1 PETER 1:6–7 (NLT)

※ ※ ※

This is just too much for me, and yet, it causes
me to lay down my self-effort and take you up
on your grace and mercy, heavenly Father. How
else could I learn to stop being so self-reliant?
I see the good in it all. I'm glad to be coming to
the end of my do-it-yourself ways and discovering
the ways of trust in your goodness and strength.
Thank you for this purging of my faith. I am
truly glad for it.

※ ※ ※

Refining our faith means taking the hard metal
of our soul and liquefying it, rendering it slack
and seemingly useless for a time, so that it can
be made over again, made less an alloy and
more pure faith itself.

❧ ❧ ❧

I guess these frustrations and trials are here for a reason, Lord. Maybe they're here to teach me to trust you, to keep me near you, and to help me grow in patience and peace. I can think of plenty of reasons you might have me in this place right now, but only you know for sure. Help me keep my focus on you and choose the right attitude minute by minute.

Rejoicing seems really impossible given my circumstances, but I can rejoice in the hope of what lies ahead. Patience is a struggle, but you will give me your Spirit of patience as I look to you for strength and courage. Remaining in a prayerful mindset is something I feel I need to continually do, so help me keep praying. Thank you, Lord. In Jesus' name, I pray. Amen.

❈ ❈ ❈

CHAPTER 5

WHEN YOU'RE FIGHTING ILLNESS

✳ ✳ ✳

My child, pay attention to what I say.
Listen carefully to my words.
Don't lose sight of them.
Let them penetrate deep
into your heart,
for they bring life to those
who find them,
and healing to their whole body.

PROVERBS 4:20–22 (NLT)

Bless the Lord, O my soul,
    and do not forget all his benefits—
Who forgives all your iniquity,
    who heals all your diseases.

PSALM 103:2–3

※ ※ ※

Lord God,
I do bring you blessing and praise, even in my
time of illness. I thank you for the many benefits
you have brought to my life—the love of family
and friends and a faith that has anchored me
through the many storms. Now I ask you for
healing that is both physical and spiritual. Let
me grow in my reliance on you even as you knit
this body back to health.

Have thine own way, Lord.
Have thine own way.
Wounded and weary, help me I pray.
Power, all power, surely is thine.
Touch me and heal me, Savior divine.

—ADELAIDE A. POLLARD,
"HAVE THINE OWN WAY"

❈ ❈ ❈

Even youths will faint and be weary,
  and the young will fall exhausted;
but those who wait for the Lord shall
  renew their strength,
they shall mount up with wings
  like eagles.

ISAIAH 40:30–31

❈ ❈ ❈

*Eagles' wings. That's what I want, dear Lord.
According to your promise, let me not just walk
or run but soar. Give me the strength to do
your bidding in amazing ways—not just
doing kind deeds, but showing the depth of
your compassion to others; not just saying nice
words, but uttering your blessing upon those
around me. I have been waiting for your healing
touch, and I admit that the wait has been
difficult, but now I look for renewed strength.
Give me a spiritual power that radiates, so that
everyone around me will know that you are
with me.*

Afflictions are but the shadow of God's wings.

—GEORGE MACDONALD

❋ ❋ ❋

A cheerful heart is a good medicine,
but a downcast spirit dries up
the bones.

PROVERBS 17:22

❋ ❋ ❋

It's hard to keep a cheerful heart when I'm laid up like this, but I'll try, heavenly Father. I'll focus on the blessings you've given me, the great memories of good times, the strong sense of your presence, and the encouraging words of those who truly care about me. There is joy in these thoughts that gets me through the pain and uncertainty. Please stay close beside me, Lord, and cheer me up when I need it.

Earth has no sorrow that heaven cannot heal.

—Thomas Moore

※ ※ ※

Therefore confess your sins to one
another, and pray for one another,
so that you may be healed.
The prayer of the righteous is
powerful and effective.

James 5:16

※ ※ ※

The Word of the Father, who made man, cares
for the entire being of his creature;
the all-sufficient Physician of humanity,
the Savior, heals both body and soul.

—Clement of Alexandria

※ ※ ※

Most merciful Lord God, I come before you in humility and in need. I cannot demand healing. I can't say that I deserve it. But I rely on your kindness and mercy. As a sinner who depends on your grace, I ask you for every kind of healing you can give me. Forgive my sins. Draw me closer to you. Restore my relationships with others. Give me hope for the future. And please, if you can find it in your will, bring my body back to health so that I can continue to serve you on this earth. I will be eternally grateful—and I mean that—for whatever renewal you choose to bring me. I will forever praise you.

Do not be wise in your own eyes;
> fear the Lord, and turn away from evil.
It will be a healing for your flesh
> and a refreshment for your body.

PROVERBS 3:7–8

※ ※ ※

Sin can lead to sickness, but sickness often
leads us closer to God. Don't assume
that sickness is punishment.
Instead, seize the opportunity it provides.

※ ※ ※

Blessed be…the Father of mercies
and the God of all consolation,
who consoles us in all our affliction,
so that we may be able to console
those who are in any affliction.

2 CORINTHIANS 1:3–4

Sometimes the Bible makes it seem too easy.
Lord, you know the respect I have for your Word,
but occasionally it seems to tell me that doing the
right thing will keep me healthy. And that makes
me wonder what horrible sin I committed that
has made me terribly sick. Then other Scriptures
remind me that Job, Paul, and others suffered
sickness through no particular fault of their
own and that comforts me somewhat. Anyway,
I'm still trying to sort this all out. I know that
disobedience is bad for me in a lot of ways, and
obedience brings many blessings—physical,
spiritual, and relational. But I also know that
even your closest friends sometimes suffer. So
please, heavenly Father, keep teaching me during
this trying time.

※ ※ ※

God of comfort, help me lift my eyes and look beyond myself. What people around me are in need of your consolation? Have you given me this difficult experience to equip me to help them? Are there other ailing people who will listen to me because I know what they're going through? Are there people visiting me who are troubled by worries and fears? Are there doctors and nurses who are overworked and who desperately need a moment of joy or a word of love? Show me these needs and how I can meet them.

※ ※ ※

Sorrow is a fruit;
God does not allow it to grow on a branch
that is too weak to bear it.

—Victor Hugo

※ ※ ※

We have this treasure in clay jars,
so that it may be made clear that this
extraordinary power belongs to God
and does not come from us.

2 Corinthians 4:7

❈ ❈ ❈

We are afflicted in every way,
but not crushed; . . . struck down,
but not destroyed; always carrying
in the body the death of Jesus,
so that the life of Jesus may also be
made visible in our bodies.

2 Corinthians 4:8–10

That's what this body is, dear Lord, a clay jar.
You scooped up some mud in Eden and fashioned
it into a human being, and you breathed into it
the breath of life. That's the heritage I hold in this
bag of bones, this motley collection of organs
that sometimes work effectively. The question,
I guess, is what's inside this jar? It's your breath,
your Spirit, that still blows through it, giving
life and power that we could never muster
ourselves. Lord, this clay jar of mine isn't much,
but I'm partial to it. I look forward to a whole
new eternal existence with you, but in the
meantime, could you patch up this jar a little?
I'll be sure to give you all the glory.

Nothing fancy about clay jars,
but they're not useless. How do archaeologists
learn about life in ancient society?
From shards of clay jars they dig up.
Turns out those broken bits have
a story to tell—and so do we.

❋ ❋ ❋

You've been here, Lord, in my shoes,
In my bones and aching sinews.
You know what it's like to be
Part of broken humanity.

❋ ❋ ❋

God did not say: "You will not be troubled,"
or "You will not be tempted," or
"You will not be distressed."
He said, "You will not be overcome."

—Julian of Norwich

We do not lose heart. Even though our outer nature is wasting away, our inner nature is being renewed day by day. For this slight momentary affliction is preparing us for an eternal weight of glory beyond all measure.

2 Corinthians 4:16–17

❈ ❈ ❈

God of glory, please renew me. I am losing heart, but you can revive my spirits. Remind me of the great promises that lie ahead. As I carry on this physical battle, whisper to me about the whole new dimension that awaits me. Let me know, Lord, that this is a temporary setback within an eternal journey of joy. Prepare me for that glorious life to come.

❈ ❈ ❈

Christ Jesus, I am honored to bear your name, and I'm continually learning what it means to be a Christian. I carry your death with me, so that I can display your life. As I struggle through this earthly existence, I am well aware that you struggled too. You weren't satisfied to stay in heavenly comfort, but you poured yourself into the human predicament, and you died. That vulnerability, that commitment, that love is something I can embody. Even as I suffer, I understand that you know this pain well. Yet I also rejoice that you rose from the grave, bringing us into a new, abundant, eternal life—a life I can proclaim and demonstrate. People will see that there is joy and hope even in suffering. Thank you, dear Jesus, for your love and life. Display them boldly in me.

❈ ❈ ❈

For you who revere my name the sun
of righteousness shall rise, with healing
in its wings. You shall go out leaping
like calves from the stall.

MALACHI 4:2

※ ※ ※

*Lord of light, rise like the sun upon me. Spread
your healing rays over me and restore me to
health and happiness. I've been sinking into
darkness, unsure of where I was going, worrying
that no one cared. But you can revive me. I want
the physical strength to get up out of bed and
skip through life like a newborn calf. Yet I also
need spiritual reviving. Let my spirit laugh
and dance too. Bring a new vibrancy to my
relationships. Let me spread sunshine to those
in my life.*

※ ※ ※

Sometimes a light surprises
The Christian while he sings;
It is the Lord who rises
With healing in his wings;
When comforts are declining,
He grants the soul again
A season of clear shining
To cheer it after rain.

—WILLIAM COWPER,
OLNEY HYMNS

※ ※ ※

Lord Jesus,

I thank you for the sacrifice you made. You came to earth to bear our sins and take our punishment upon yourself. I am awed by the magnitude of the love it took to do that. Isaiah speaks about the "infirmities" and "diseases" you took upon yourself in order to heal us. Those words carry special meaning for me now in my own time of illness. It makes me appreciate all the more what you went through, willingly taking on the sickness of the human race. I know that the healing you offer is more than just bodily. You are loosening sin's grip on us, healing our hearts as well as our hurts. And so I praise you, the great Healer. Please continue to work your wonders in me. I pray in your precious name. Amen.

※ ※ ※

Surely he has borne our infirmities
and carried our diseases...
But he was wounded for our
transgressions, crushed for our
iniquities; upon him was the
punishment that made us whole,
and by his bruises we are healed.

ISAIAH 53:4–5

※ ※ ※

There is a balm in Gilead to make
the wounded whole;
there is a balm in Gilead to heal
the sin-sick soul.

—TRADITIONAL SPIRITUAL,
BASED ON JEREMIAH 8:22

※ ※ ※

Because he himself was tested by what
he suffered, he is able to help those
who are being tested.

HEBREWS 2:18

※ ※ ※

*If this is a test, my Lord, I'm not sure I'll earn
a passing grade. As I fight this illness, I am tired
and cranky and hurting and worried. I'm not
a lot of fun to be with right now, but I take some
comfort from the thought that you are still with
me. When I complain, you know exactly what
I'm talking about, because you've been through
it too. Stay close beside me, dear Lord. I need your
empathetic touch.*

※ ※ ※

Just when we cry,
"I can't take it anymore,"
Jesus is there to say,
"I know, I care, I did, you can."

❋ ❋ ❋

Oh, restore me to health and make
    me live!...
The living, the living, they
    thank you,
    as I do this day.

ISAIAH 38:16, 19

❋ ❋ ❋

Lord of life, it's life I ask of you—life brimming with energy, full of relationships, and active with good deeds. This is the kind of life I want to return to. I know it's a bit of a cliché to bargain with you in a time of need—"If you heal me, I'll be the best person ever!"—but this sickness has helped me appreciate health all the more. If you restore me to a productive life, I will exult in it. I won't waste it. I will live fully and freely and fabulously for your glory.

※ ※ ※

This illness does not lead to death;
rather it is for God's glory, so that the
Son of God may be glorified through it.

JOHN 11:4

※ ※ ※

The glory of God is someone fully alive.

—IRENAEUS

※ ※ ※

Dear Jesus,
When you walked this earth, you were a healer,
and that fact offers me hope. I trust that you
can still bring healing to my life for your glory.
I know that your healings in the Bible had
a special purpose to prove your power and
demonstrate your divine identity, but why can't
that happen here now? I am praying for healing,
and everyone I know recognizes that fact. If
you heal me, they will know how great you are
and how gracious you can be. I trust you to do
something amazing in my life, and I wait eagerly
to see what that is.

※ ※ ※

He heals those that are broken in heart and
gives medicine to heal their sickness.

—ADAPTED FROM
BOOK OF COMMON PRAYER

※ ※ ※

Rash words are like sword thrusts,
but the tongue of the wise brings
healing.

PROVERBS 12:18

※ ※ ※

When you don't know what to say,
start with a tear, a smile, a touch, a hug.
Then maybe a few choice words will arise,
or maybe they won't need to.

※ ※ ※

Dear Lord,

I'm becoming aware of how important words are, especially in times of suffering. I think of Job's friends, who apparently were trying to help but were full of accusation. I have some friends like that too. Then there are those who say beautiful words of comfort. It's not that the words are expertly crafted, but I know they come from hearts that care deeply for me. I thank you for these friends and their words. I also ask you to keep me from polluting my language with too many complaints. Help me say words that bring healing to others.

※ ※ ※

Heal me, O Lord, and I will be healed;
save me and I will be saved,
for you are the one I praise.

JEREMIAH 17:14 (NIV)

※ ※ ※

Heal us, Emmanuel, hear our prayer;
we wait to feel thy touch;
Deep-wounded souls to thee repair,
and Savior, we are such.

—WILLIAM COWPER,
"HEAL US, EMMANUEL"

※ ※ ※

Dear God,

I need healing in many forms. Physical illness is ravaging me, but my attitude's not very good, and some of my closest relationships are sadly fraying. My heart is weighed down with constant worry. My spirit is sore. In my need, I come to you, the great Healer. Start your work of restoration within me, and I will praise you as long as I live. In Jesus' name, I pray. Amen.

※ ※ ※

CHAPTER 6

WHEN YOU'RE STRUGGLING WITH LONELINESS

❈ ❈ ❈

Whom the heart of man shuts out, Sometimes the heart of God takes in, And fences them all round about With silence mid the world's loud din.

—JAMES RUSSELL LOWELL, "THE FORLORN"

Turn to me and be gracious to me,
for I am lonely and afflicted.

PSALM 25:16

※ ※ ※

Dear Lord,
The comforts of human companionship feel far,
far away. I don't want to be alone, but I am. It's
only because I know you're here that I'm not lost
in this abyss of loneliness. I'm definitely going to
need to keep talking to you; help me trust that
you're hearing me. And please, I pray, grant me
a sense of your presence with me. Thank you for
being here.

※ ※ ※

A solitude is the audience-chamber of God.

—WALTER SAVAGE LANDOR

※ ※ ※

A father to the fatherless, a defender
of widows, is God in his holy dwelling.
God sets the lonely in families.

PSALM 68:5–6 (NIV)

It feels like a kind of spiritual and emotional nakedness, divine Father, to be left without someone here to defend and watch out for me in this world. I'm not used to this. I feel insecure and vulnerable. Please come and cover me with your protection, with your provision, and with your presence. I cry out to you to take my hand and lead me to safety and security. Surround me with people who will be kind and compassionate, helpful and loving. Send them in your grace and in your wisdom, as you see fit. Help me look to you for everything I need, now and ever. In Jesus' name, I pray.

❈ ❈ ❈

It is loneliness that makes the loudest noise. This is as true of men as of dogs.

—ERIC HOFFER

❈ ❈ ❈

Children of the heavenly Father
Safely in His bosom gather;
Nestling bird nor star in heaven
Such a refuge e'er was given.

—CAROLINA V. S. BERG

❈ ❈ ❈

I am like an owl of the wilderness,
like a little owl of the waste places.
I lie awake; I am like a lonely bird
on the housetop.

PSALM 102:6–7

Being alone is swallowing me up, heavenly Father! If only I could escape my loneliness in sleep, but it is so painful that it even keeps me awake at night. I can hear my own heart beating: "A-lone, a-lone, a-lone." How am I supposed to get through this? How do I stop feeling this way? I'm like a helpless child, longing for the rescue of a parent. I keep wondering how much longer? I just don't know; there is no relief in sight. But I'll keep looking to you. I know you hear me. Thank you for always being there for me.

❈ ❈ ❈

The Lord is good to those whose
hope is in him, to the one who seeks
him; it is good to wait quietly for
the salvation of the Lord.

LAMENTATIONS 3:25–26 (NIV)

❈ ❈ ❈

Dear Lord,

I wasn't ready to lose this friend! The truth is, I never would have been ready, not in a hundred lifetimes. But you know that, and my real reason for coming to you now is to ask you why. Why this friend? Why now? I know I won't find the answers this side of heaven, but I can't help asking. There's such a great void now, where my friend was standing. O, I just want you to come and bring your comfort to me. How my heart aches! Even so, I look to the consolation of that day when we will be reunited—my friend and I—as ones who have been saved by your grace. So stay near to me, dear Savior, during the rest of my journey in this world. In your most holy name, I pray.

❊ ❊ ❊

Being committed to you and your ways brings its own kind of loneliness in this world, my Lord. I feel like an alien, a stranger, so much of the time. Because your Holy Spirit lives in me, the things I'm drawn to are not the things of this world anymore. I often have to part company with others because my loves and loyalties are toward you. The solitude of serving you, the loneliness of obedience, the quietness of listening and waiting: These are part of belonging to you. Teach me to embrace them and be taught by them according to your purposes for me.

※ ※ ※

Be good and you will be lonesome.

—MARK TWAIN

'Tis sweet, as year by year we lose
Friends out of sight, in faith to muse
How grows in Paradise our store.

—JOHN KEBLE,
"BURIAL OF THE DEAD"

⁂ ⁂ ⁂

It is good for one to bear the yoke
in youth, to sit alone in silence when
the Lord has imposed it.

LAMENTATIONS 3:27–28

⁂ ⁂ ⁂

The widow who is really in need and
left all alone puts her hope in God and
continues night and day to pray and to
ask God for help.

1 TIMOTHY 5:5 (NIV)

⁂ ⁂ ⁂

Heavenly Father,
Thank you for the place you have in your heart
for women bereaved of their husbands. You make
provision in your church for each one who is in
need. You take a special interest in the welfare
and well-being of those who put their trust
in you. May you bring true comfort in their
loneliness, even as you provide for their physical
needs. In Jesus' name. Amen.

※ ※ ※

God gives us love. Something to love
He lends us; but when love is grown
To ripeness, that on which it throve
Falls off, and love is left alone.

—ALFRED TENNYSON

※ ※ ※

He is despised and rejected of men;
a man of sorrows, and acquainted
with grief: and we hid as it were our
faces from him; he was despised,
and we esteemed him not.

ISAIAH 53:3 (KJV)

✕ ✕ ✕

Dear Jesus,
You felt loneliness as it has never been experienced
before. Sometimes I forget that you understand,
not just in some special cosmic way, but as a real
life experience. You weren't just generally lonely;
you were hated, rejected, and often grieved.
When I remember that, I can imagine you sitting
next to me with your quiet empathy and with
your heart of understanding holding my longing
soul. How meaningful your love is, how real
and true!

When Christ said: "I was hungry
and you fed me," he didn't mean only
the hunger for bread and for food;
he also meant the hunger to be loved.
Jesus himself experienced this loneliness.
He came amongst his own and his own received
him not, and it hurt him then and it has kept
on hurting him. The same hunger, the same
loneliness, the same having no one to be
accepted by and to be loved and
wanted by. Every human being in that
case resembles Christ in his loneliness;
and that is the hardest part, that's real hunger.

—MOTHER TERESA,
A GIFT FOR GOD

❋ ❋ ❋

If my father and mother forsake me,
the Lord will take me up.

PSALM 27:10

It's hard to imagine that you have a purpose for me while I'm in this valley of loneliness. It's even harder to think that the loneliness itself might have some meaning. But, heavenly Father, you have been faithful to me over my lifetime, even when I've been unfaithful. The reality of your presence here is only augmented by the lack of others to distract my attention from it. So I guess there really may be some good that can come out of this time of being alone. Yet, please keep me from growing despondent and frustrated as I wait for your purposes and your plan to unfold.

⁂ ⁂ ⁂

Though He giveth or He taketh,
God His children ne'er forsaketh,
His the loving purpose solely
To preserve them pure and holy.

—CAROLINA V. S. BERG

※ ※ ※

Then the Lord God said, "It is not good
that the man should be alone; I will
make him a helper as his partner."

GENESIS 2:18

※ ※ ※

Holy God, you made us to be in relationship.
Why, then, do you sometimes call me to lonely
places? Are there things that I can only learn in
solitude, just as there are some things that I can
only learn in relationship? If this is so, please help
me be a quick learner in this loneliness. And yet,
if the lesson is to learn to love your presence more,
I will be learning to let the loneliness linger. How
strange and wonderful is your wisdom! Here is
my hand; please lead on.

※ ※ ※

Two people are better off than one, for
they can help each other succeed. If
one person falls, the other can reach
out and help.

ECCLESIASTES 4:9–10 (NLT)

※ ※ ※

Divine Father,
I am alone right now, but I long for friendship.
Please lead me into relationships that will be
pleasing to you, that will be mutually beneficial,
and that will cause me to grow in truth and love.
Help me listen to your voice as you guide me
into the friendships you have for me. Thank you
for the gift of friendships.

※ ※ ※

No one would choose a friendless existence
on condition of having all the other
things in the world.

—ARISTOTLE,
NICOMACHEAN ETHICS

❈ ❈ ❈

Ah, Jesus!

*You stood in my place when you were all alone
on that cross—even forsaken by your Father.
Now I can be accepted by him because of your
selfless gift of substitution. You've made a way
for me to be forever in relationship with your
Father, who now calls me his own child.
Thanking you hardly seems enough, but my
heart will be eternally full of gratitude to you.
I love you.*

❈ ❈ ❈

About three o'clock Jesus cried with a loud voice, "Eli, Eli, lema sabachthani?" that is, "My God, my God, why have you forsaken me?"

MATTHEW 27:46

※ ※ ※

What language shall I borrow
To thank Thee, dearest Friend,
For this Thy dying sorrow,
Thy pity without end?
Oh, make me Thine forever;
And should I fainting be,
Lord, let me never, never
Outlive my love to Thee.

—BERNARD OF CLAIRVAUX

※ ※ ※

Upon you I have leaned from my
birth; it was you who took me from
my mother's womb.... Do not cast
me off in the time of old age; do not
forsake me when my strength is spent.

PSALM 71:6, 9

❈ ❈ ❈

*At this stage of my life, as I am growing older,
I feel a deep loneliness that I had not experienced
nor contemplated before. Losing companions,
parents, friends, and others along the way has
begun to thin what was once a thick forest of
relationships in my life. There are gaps now over
which lie shadows of sorrow and regret, pain and
longing. Please be with me, my Lord, and stay
with me as I move forward into these later years.
I'll need your arm to lean on more than ever now.*

❈ ❈ ❈

Our times are in His hand
Who saith, "A whole I planned,
Youth shows but half; trust God:
see all nor be afraid!"

—ROBERT BROWNING,
"RABBI BEN EZRA"

✳ ✳ ✳

Do not forsake your friend or the
friend of your parent.... Better is a
neighbor who is nearby than kindred
who are far away.

PROVERBS 27:10

✳ ✳ ✳

I'm very lonely now, . . .
For the poor make no new friends;
But oh they love the better still
The few our Father sends!

—HELEN SELINA, LADY DUFFERIN SHERIDAN,
"LAMENT OF THE IRISH EMIGRANT"

Dear God,

Sometimes I try to dictate to you how my friends should come, what they should be like, and whether or not I'll accept some of the people you send my way as candidates for friendship. I admit I've brought some of my loneliness upon myself by rejecting others because of my own "standards" and "tastes." Help me value others the way you do and give people a fair and fighting chance to share some aspect of my life. Not everyone needs to be "best friend" material for me to enjoy their company and uniqueness. Also help me value the friends I have already, Lord, and let them know how much I love and appreciate them. Thank you for each one. They are truly a blessing to me in so many wonderful ways.

※ ※ ※

Remind me, dear Lord,
That when friends fail me, that I have sometimes
failed others as well. Remind me, too, Lord,
that you've never failed me and that you've
helped me entrust myself to you when I felt alone
or abandoned. Comfort my heart when I feel
betrayed or forgotten. Fill me with a gift of grace
and forgiveness for those who I feel have let me
down. Teach me to communicate in loving and
healing ways as I seek to fortify bruised or broken
relationships. Thank you that you are forever
with me and that the message of your gospel,
of your love flowing through me, will go forward
no matter what others may or may not do.

※ ※ ※

At my first defense no one stood with me,
but all forsook me.... But the Lord
stood with me and strengthened me,
so that the message might be preached
fully through me.

2 Timothy 4:16–17 (NKJV)

❊❊ ❊❊ ❊❊

Abide with me—fast falls the eventide;
The darkness deepens—Lord, with me abide!
When other helpers fail and comforts flee,
Help of the helpless, oh, abide with me.

—Henry F. Lyte, "Abide with Me"

❊❊ ❊❊ ❊❊

It is the Lord who goes before you;
he will be with you, he will not fail you
or forsake you; do not fear or be
dismayed.

DEUTERONOMY 31:8 (RSV)

※ ※ ※

This is new territory, and I feel nervous to take the next step. People are skeptical, and I haven't found much encouragement, but it seems clear that you are pointing in this direction. I'm afraid of failing, and of being wrong. But, Lord, even if I am wrong, even if I do fail, you won't forsake me. If I don't go forward, I will feel as if I've not done what you're calling me to do, so I need to do this. Please keep me from a wrong path, but most of all, keep me near you and be my guide. I'll keep trusting you even in this seeming darkness. Thank you, Lord!

I would rather walk with God in the dark
than go alone in the light.

—MARY GARDINER BRAINARD,
NOT KNOWING

❀ ❀ ❀

The Lord is a stronghold ... in times
of trouble. And those who know your
name put their trust in you, for you,
O Lord, have not forsaken those who
seek you.

PSALM 9:9–10

❀ ❀ ❀

Under His wings I am safely abiding;
Though the night deepens and
tempests are wild,
Still I can trust Him,
I know He will keep me;
He has redeemed me,
and I am His child.

—William O. Cushing,
"Under His Wings"

✵ ✵ ✵

Dear Jesus,

Things seem to have gone crazy in my life, and I'm out of reach of all of my loved ones! They're either too far away or too overwhelmed with their own lives to be of much help to me right now. There's no one to blame; it's all situational, but, Lord, I need help, and there's no one! But there is you, and you are more than enough. I'm throwing myself on you, asking you to grant me strength, wisdom, and resources. And most of all please grant me the nearness of your presence. Thank you for this trial that will draw me near to you once again as I lean into your love. In your name, I pray. Amen.

※ ※ ※

CHAPTER 7

WHEN YOU'RE
HAVING
RELATIONAL
STRIFE

❊ ❊ ❊

I give you a new commandment,
that you love one another.
Just as I have loved you,
you also should love one another.
By this everyone will know
that you are my disciples,
if you have love for one another.

JOHN 13:34–35

Bear with one another and, if anyone has a complaint against another, forgive each other; just as the Lord has forgiven you, so you also must forgive.

COLOSSIANS 3:13

※ ※ ※

The one who forgives ends the quarrel.

—AFRICAN PROVERB

※ ※ ※

You shall not take vengeance or bear a grudge against any of your people, but you shall love your neighbor as yourself.

LEVITICUS 19:18

※ ※ ※

Dear Lord,

I'm still trying to figure out forgiveness. It goes against everything I feel right now. I've been wronged—you and I both know that—but now I'm supposed to act as if everything's fine? All right, Lord, I realize that this is exactly what you've done for me—forgiven me. Yes, I know I've done plenty of wrong things to hurt you and you have mercifully wiped the slate clean. But somehow that's a theological transaction, and the issue I'm struggling with now is very personal. How can I forgive this person who has caused me so much grief? How can I even look at that person? It will take some sort of miracle to do that; I'm pretty sure I can't do that on my own. So if that's what you want from me, Lord, please help me do that.

❊❊❊ ❊❊❊ ❊❊❊

Prince of Peace, my heart is clenched tight as I come before you. I admit that I'm holding a grudge. This is born of deep hurt and overwhelming pain caused by an uncaring person. I can't seem to go an hour without thinking of the injury I've suffered, and each time I do, my heart glazes over again, hardening a little more. "Love your neighbor as yourself." That sounded so easy when I learned it as a child. Now it seems impossible. My heart is a rock, weighing heavier each day. Please soften it.

※ ※ ※

Beloved Lord,

I pray today for my family, not only the family that shares my DNA but also those who share my faith. As you know, families are complicated, and I've told you plenty about my daily problems with this one or that one. Expectations run high. Wounds run deep. There are dysfunctions that only you can unravel, and so I ask you to bring your wisdom and power into those situations. And I also pray for those caring friends who have gathered around me as a second family. Thank you for their support, and I ask you to support them in their various needs. Let love reign in my home and in my heart. This is my deepest prayer. Amen.

❖ ❖ ❖

Love the family you're given,
but gather the family you need.

※ ※ ※

A grudge weighs heaviest in the hand
of the one who holds it.

※ ※ ※

[Jesus] said to them, "My mother and
my brothers are those who hear the
word of God and do it."

LUKE 8:21

※ ※ ※

Do not judge, and you will not be
judged; do not condemn,
and you will not be condemned.
Forgive, and you will be forgiven;
give, and it will be given to you.

LUKE 6:37–38

Sovereign God, it isn't easy being your deputy here on earth. I mean, if I don't let people know when they fall short of your desires, who will? Oh, of course, the Holy Spirit will, but isn't it my responsibility to help? Isn't it? You can't really expect me to suspend judgment when the people around me are being blatantly sinful. I know I'm sinful too, but I'm aware of my sins, so that's different, isn't it? Are you really asking me to forgive? But then what happens to standards of righteousness? Who will uphold those standards? I don't know, Lord. I'm having trouble with this whole forgiveness thing. Please help me out here.

❈ ❈ ❈

You must bear with me.
Pray you now, forget and forgive.

—SHAKESPEARE, *KING LEAR*

Do not fret because of the wicked;
do not be envious of wrongdoers,
for they will soon fade like the grass....
Commit your way to the Lord;
trust in him, and he will act.

PSALM 37:1, 2, 5

✳ ✳ ✳

Please, Lord, step into this situation. I don't know what to do. Things were done, words were said, and now I'm at odds with someone. Maybe I was wrong, but I don't think so. Honestly I want to blame the other person for all of it, but maybe I have a blind spot. I want to sort things out and turn things around, but I'm not sure where to start. I don't know if a half-baked apology will do any good, especially if I don't really mean it. And actually I should be receiving an apology, but I doubt that will ever happen. Anyway, I beg you, please do your work here. Shine your light so we see things clearly. Use your power to dismantle whatever grudges we have piled up. I commit this whole mess to you.

※ ※ ※

Determining who's mostly to blame is like slicing pudding. It's best to just share it all.

Let us not grow weary in doing what
is right.... So then, whenever we have
an opportunity, let us work for the
good of all, and especially for those
of the family of faith.

GALATIANS 6:9–10

❊ ❊ ❊

*I'll admit it, dear Lord, sometimes I do get weary.
I try to show your love to others—by caring,
by giving, and by going the extra mile. But those
extra miles add up. There are a lot of people who
take advantage of my kindness. They assume
I won't mind doing extra work, giving them
a ride, or rescheduling my life around theirs.
That's just the way I am. But I have to tell you,
Lord, I'm tired of it. Please give me some extra
strength soon, or I'm just going to shut down.
Please help me!*

And throughout all eternity
I forgive you, you forgive me.
As our dear Redeemer said:
"This the wine and this the bread."

—WILLIAM BLAKE

❊ ❊ ❊

Little children, let us love, not in word
or speech, but in truth and action.

1 JOHN 3:18

❊ ❊ ❊

Most holy God,
I bow before you today in introspection and
confession. I talk a good game, but I don't
always live up to it. I say loving words, but my
actions don't match. I have acted selfishly and
inconsiderately. I've been more interested in
my own pleasure than in the welfare of others.
For this I am truly sorry, and I humbly repent.
Please help me patch up the relationships I have
damaged.

It's not the loving words you say.
It's the things you do each day.

Blessed are the merciful,
for they will receive mercy.

MATTHEW 5:7

Great God,
I am in awe of the mercy you have shown me.
Though I have sinned, you have forgiven me, and
you offer a rich, abundant life. Daily I realize
the gifts that you shower upon me, and I am
deeply thankful. Now help me show that mercy
to others. Let me respond to curses with blessings
and to mistreatment with prayer. Let me love
others with your amazing love.

※ ※ ※

Do you find it hard to show mercy to someone
who doesn't deserve it? No one deserves mercy.
That's the whole point.

※ ※ ※

Blessed are the peacemakers,
for they will be called children of God.

MATTHEW 5:9

O Lord, I want to be a peacemaker. I know that's a challenging task in this strife-ridden world, but you have the power to endow me with this trait. Everybody loves peace, but creating it is tough. To listen, to care, to put another person's needs ahead of your own, and to master the soft answer—these are skills I'm still working on, but I aspire to. In your goodness, Lord, help me grow in peacemaking. Let me begin with ending the quarrels currently brewing around me. Help me bring both heart and mind to the conflict so that I might exude love and find creative solutions.

※ ※ ※

Where cross the crowded ways of life,
Where sound the cries of race and clan,
Above the noise of selfish strife,
We hear your voice, O Son of Man.

—FRANK MASON NORTH,
"WHERE CROSS THE CROWDED WAYS OF LIFE"

※ ※ ※

Love is patient; love is kind; love is
not envious or boastful or arrogant or
rude. It does not insist on its own way;
it is not irritable or resentful.

1 CORINTHIANS 13:4–5

※ ※ ※

I want a love with feet to walk your road,
A love with serving hands.
I want a love with eyes to see your need,
And a heart that understands.

Lead me, my Lord, through this current conflict.
I know there's a way, and I trust you to show me.
It will be a way of patience and kindness, where
I put down the "rights" I think I deserve and
truly consider my opponent's needs. It will be a
way of openness and vulnerability. Of course,
I find that scary, but I know it's the way we need
to go. Go with me, dear Lord. Lead the way.

※ ※ ※

Let love be genuine...
Live in harmony with one another...
Do not repay anyone evil for evil,
but take thought for what is noble
in the sight of all.

ROMANS 12:9, 16—17

※ ※ ※

What troubles have we seen,
what mighty conflicts past,
Fightings without and fears within,
since we assembled last.
Yet out of all the Lord hath brought us
by his love,
And still he doth his help afford,
and hides our life above.

—CHARLES WESLEY,
"AND ARE WE YET ALIVE"

❋ ❋ ❋

Putting away falsehood, let all of us
speak the truth to our neighbors....
Be angry but do not sin; do not let the
sun go down on your anger.

Ephesians 4:25–26

※ ※ ※

Loving God, fill me with your kind of love.
Not the sappy, first-sight, skin-deep puppy love
I see in the movies. I'm talking about robust
compassion, tough love, knock-down-drag-out
commitment. I want a love that doesn't run from
honesty and a love that sees and serves the value
in another soul. Give me a love that transforms
situations, that transforms people, and that
transforms me.

※ ※ ※

Let no evil talk come out of your mouths, but only what is useful for building up, as there is need, so that your words may give grace to those who hear.

EPHESIANS 4:29

※ ※ ※

To err is human, to forgive divine.

—ALEXANDER POPE

※ ※ ※

Beloved, let us love one another, because love is from God; everyone who loves is born of God and knows God.

1 JOHN 4:7

※ ※ ※

O Lord,

You know I'm angry. I am burning with a desire
for revenge. I have been royally mistreated,
and I'm looking for major payback. If you don't
hold me back, I'm going to hurt someone....
All right, let me breathe a little. You're telling me
to slow down, to keep control of the situation,
and to seek resolution rather than revenge. That's
difficult, Lord. You're asking me to communicate,
to confront, and to mend a relationship with
words rather than hiding behind my fists. Will
that really work? If I give that a try, will you
go with me? You'll have to give me the right
words to say, because I have no clue what they
are. And, through your Holy Spirit, keep
breathing in me, so I can let this anger out.

※ ※ ※

Dear God,

I want my words to bless, but oh so often they curse. I want to speak comfort, but it is challenge that comes out. Empower me to control my tongue so that my language builds people up rather than tearing them down. Help me look for the good and comment on that rather than the bad. Let me soothe conflict rather than sparking it. Guide me in my thinking and talking so that grace emanates from my life toward all around me. Let them hear your compassion coming out of my mouth.

※ ※ ※

O fill me with thy fullness, Lord,
until my very heart o'erflow
In kindling thought and glowing word,
thy love to tell, thy praise to show.

—FRANCES R. HAVERGAL,
"LORD, SPEAK TO ME"

※ ※ ※

Whoever wants to be first must be
last of all and servant of all.

MARK 9:35

※ ※ ※

Bow, stubborn knees,
and heart with strings of steel.
Be soft as sinews of the newborn babe.

—SHAKESPEARE, *HAMLET*

Lord Jesus,

You are my example. You came not to be served but to serve. You gave your very life for us. Even though you were God, you didn't cling to those privileges, but you humbled yourself. You knelt to wash the feet of your disciples, and you challenged all of us to do the same. Yet I find myself in conflict with others. I wish that others would follow your example of servanthood; that would make my life much easier. But I recognize that my me-first attitude doesn't help much either. I need more than your example; I need your strength to bend my knees, to loosen my clinging fingers, and to soften my proud heart. Help me be a better servant. I pray in your precious name. Amen.

❋ ❋ ❋

Hatred stirs up strife,
but love covers all offenses.

PROVERBS 10:12

※ ※ ※

The change has to start in my heart, heavenly Father. I can say the words and go through the motions, but I know that won't heal this relationship. I need to commit myself to love, thoroughly and completely. I can't reserve a corner of my heart for grudge-holding. I can't nurse my hurt under the surface. I need to do the hard work of forgiving, of understanding, of caring, and of giving. For that to happen, I need you to walk beside me, every step of the way.

※ ※ ※

Help us to help each other, Lord,
each other's cross to bear;
Let all their friendly aid afford,
and feel each other's care.

—CHARLES WESLEY,
"JESUS, UNITED BY THY GRACE"

Then Peter came to him and asked,
"Lord, how often should I forgive
someone who sins against me?
Seven times?"
"No, not seven times," Jesus replied,
"but seventy times seven!"

MATTHEW 18:21–22 (NLT)

※ ※ ※

The noblest vengeance is to forgive.

—ENGLISH PROVERB

※ ※ ※

Bear with one another and, if anyone
has a complaint against another,
forgive each other; just as the Lord has
forgiven you, so you also must forgive.

COLOSSIANS 3:13

※ ※ ※

I tried to forgive, dear Lord, I really did. I shrugged it off and said, "Don't worry about it." But then it happened again. And again. I'm not sure I can keep forgiving. There's a scoreboard in my heart now, and every time this person does anything I don't like, that's a tally against that person. Lord, I know I'm supposed to wipe that slate clean every time, as you did with me, but I'm not sure how. Show me. Guide me. Teach me. In Jesus' name, I pray. Amen.

⬚ ⬚ ⬚

Chapter 8

When You're Needing Forgiveness

[The prodigal son] arose,
and came to his father.
But when he was yet a great
way off, his father saw him,
and had compassion,
and ran, and fell on his neck,
and kissed him.

Luke 15:20 (KJV)

*Heavenly Father, as I read the Scriptures,
they clearly show me that extending forgiveness
is a part of your character—in fact, it's who
you are. And yet, at times I struggle to accept
your forgiveness for myself. For some reason,
it's easy for me to believe that you'd forgive
someone else's sins, but it's difficult for me to
believe you'd forgive mine. I'm not sure why
I feel this way. I guess it's because I think
my sin is somehow worse than anyone else's.
I need to learn to trust in your forgiving heart.
Help me, Lord, because I need your mercy,
fresh and new—a clean slate each and every day.
Thank you for your unfailing love toward me.
I love you!*

※ ※ ※

The Lord, the Lord, a God merciful
and gracious, slow to anger,
and abounding in steadfast love
and faithfulness, . . . forgiving iniquity
and transgression and sin.

Exodus 34:6–7

※ ※ ※

Accepting God's forgiveness reveals both our
trust in him and our gratitude toward him.

※ ※ ※

If my people who are called by my
name humble themselves, pray,
seek my face, and turn from their
wicked ways, then I will hear from
heaven, and will forgive their sin
and heal their land.

2 Chronicles 7:14

As I seek your forgiveness today, heavenly Father, let it be with a sincere heart that humbly listens to your voice of loving correction. Help me not be proud or presumptuous nor, on the other hand, self-condemning and hopeless. May I come ready to receive your forgiveness and prepared to walk in a new direction that leads to wholeness.

❋ ❋ ❋

Suit the action to the word,
the word to the action.

—SHAKESPEARE, *HAMLET*

❋ ❋ ❋

O you who answer prayer!
To you all flesh shall come.
When deeds of iniquity overwhelm us,
you forgive our transgressions.

PSALM 65:2–3

❋ ❋ ❋

Here I am again, Lord. I stumbled over the
same old thing. I'm so tired of losing this battle.
Aren't you tired of forgiving me? Aren't you
ready to give up on me? How is it that you are
willing again and again to forgive me and
take me by the hand and try one more time?
Thank you for not giving up on me, Lord!

Our weaknesses keep us near our Lord;
they remind us we will never outlive
our need for him.

※ ※ ※

Then I acknowledged my sin to you,
and I did not hide my iniquity; I said,
"I will confess my transgressions to
the Lord," and you forgave the guilt of
my sin.

PSALM 32:5

※ ※ ※

I hear my friends make excuses for my bad temper, heavenly Father. "Oh, it's just your disposition," they say. Or "It's the way you were brought up." Or "Everyone does that." I don't want to come to you with any excuses. The way I flew off the handle was inexcusable. I knew it was wrong, and I did it anyway. I ignored you and did what I wanted to do in the moment. And now, O Lord, if I could only take it back. How I regret my selfish decision! I just want to come before you and "come clean." Here I am. Please forgive me, and help me learn from this experience to do what's right next time.

※ ※ ※

Anger itself is not wrong; how and when we express it can be right or wrong; expressing it with malice is never right.

※ ※ ※

Hide thy face from my sins, and blot out all mine iniquities. Create in me a clean heart, O God; and renew a right spirit within me.

PSALM 51:9–10 (KJV)

❈ ❈ ❈

I know that my sin affects me, dear Father. It changes me. It mucks up my heart and causes me to behave in a sort of independence from you that goes from bad to worse. Not only do I need your forgiveness right now, but I also need a renewed heart and mind. Please wash away the grime of sin I've allowed to accumulate. I want to see things from your perspective again. I want to care about what is right and true and good. I want to be in close fellowship with you once more. Oh, how good it is to be renewed by you!

❈ ❈ ❈

Sin is like a parasite on our spirit,
drawing the life out of us as it grows ever larger.
That's why the sooner we're rid of it,
the better we'll be.

※ ※ ※

For as the heaven is high above the
earth, so great is [God's] mercy toward
them that fear him. As far as the east is
from the west, so far hath he removed
our transgressions from us.

PSALM 103:11–12 (KJV)

※ ※ ※

Dear Lord,

When I fear that you're holding my past sin over my head, help me remember that this fear is not based on truth. In fact, it's a flat-out lie. Your Word says Satan is an accuser of those who belong to you; help me not play into his hand by believing self-condemning lies that are contrary to your Word. Your Word says when you forgive me, you forgive me once and for all. You have removed my sins from me never to be seen again. I choose to believe your Word.

※ ※ ※

God's "do-overs" are truly
fresh starts—clean slates without even
a hint of chalk dust on them.

※ ※ ※

If you, O Lord, kept a record of sins,
O Lord, who could stand? But with
you there is forgiveness; therefore you
are feared. I wait for the Lord, my soul
waits, and in his word I put my hope.

PSALM 130:3–5 (NIV)

※ ※ ※

*At times I tend to compare myself with other
people, dear Lord, thinking I'm better or worse
than this person or that person. How futile those
thoughts are! Especially when I consider that
we're all sinners in need of your forgiveness.
It levels the playing field to think in those terms.
I'm so glad that with you there is forgiveness.
If there wasn't, what would we all—what would
I—do? Please cause my reverence for you to grow
as I humbly accept your amazing gift of mercy—
a forgiveness big enough for everyone.*

At the foot of the cross,
there is no rating system for sinners,
only a Redeemer to save them.

❖ ❖ ❖

[Lord], forgive us our sins, as we have
forgiven those who sin against us....
If you forgive those who sin against
you, your heavenly Father will
forgive you.

MATTHEW 6:12, 14 (NLT)

❖ ❖ ❖

The glory of Christianity is
to conquer by forgiveness.

—WILLIAM BLAKE,
"TO THE DEISTS," *JERUSALEM* (1804–20)

❖ ❖ ❖

May your forgiveness spur me on to forgive those around me, Lord. Help me not be stingy with extending mercy but be generous as you are. Help me forgive fully as one who has been fully forgiven. Then, Lord, may your mercy flow through me, coming full circle to remind me of how your forgiveness has set me free to forgive.

※ ※ ※

Then [Jesus] took a cup, and after
giving thanks he gave it to them,
saying, "Drink from it, all of you;
for this is my blood of the covenant,
which is poured out for many for
the forgiveness of sins."

MATTHEW 26:27–28

※ ※ ※

Dear heavenly Father,
How is it that the forgiveness I need so much
could be purchased for me by your Son's sacrifice?
The very One from whom I need forgiveness
has taken the initiative to make forgiveness
possible for me. What a powerful mystery! What
an extraordinary mercy! I receive it with my
deepest gratitude. Amen.

❋ ❋ ❋

Mercy there was great, and grace was free;
Pardon there was multiplied to me;
There my burdened soul found liberty—
At Calvary.

—WILLIAM R. NEWELL,
"AT CALVARY"

❋ ❋ ❋

When they came to the place that is called The Skull, they crucified Jesus there with the criminals, one on his right and one on his left. Then Jesus said, "Father, forgive them."

LUKE 23:33–34

As you forgave the soldiers who were torturing you, Lord, I'm also reminded of the two thieves' responses to you. One thief humbly asked you to remember him when you come into your heavenly kingdom; the other one sneered. This second thief is a haunting portrait of my own pride at times. I've come to realize that pride is sin with a capital S. It declares my independence from you and refuses to seek your forgiveness. O Lord, how foolish I am when my pride is running the show! Please, I don't want to be like that. Help me be humble. Help me recognize my desperate need for you. And help me honor you by receiving the forgiveness you extend and then extending your forgiveness to others, even to my enemies. In your name, I pray. Amen.

❈ ❈ ❈

Pride's every effort is bent
on keeping itself in view;
humility, however, simply looks up.

❈ ❈ ❈

In [Jesus] we have redemption
through his blood, the forgiveness of
sins, in accordance with the riches of
God's grace that he lavished on us with
all wisdom and understanding.

EPHESIANS 1:7–8 (NIV)

❈ ❈ ❈

If we confess our sins,
he who is faithful and just will
forgive us our sins and cleanse us
from all unrighteousness.

1 JOHN 1:9

❈ ❈ ❈

Here I am again, Lord! I need to be reassured that you're not tired of having me come to you for more forgiveness. My conscience is throbbing, and I just want to be made right with you again. I want to start over, and I also need your wisdom and insight as to how to go about making amends to this person I've harmed. I opened my mouth when I shouldn't have. I "pushed the buttons" of this one I love because I wanted to make my point more than I wanted to be in fellowship with that person. Please forgive my wrong priorities, my wrong motives, my wrong attitudes, and my wrong words. Please lavish your grace on me and on our relationship, according to your wisdom and understanding. Thank you, heavenly Father.

❋ ❋ ❋

Forgiveness is both the balm and
the glue of our relationships.

※ ※ ※

Sin has many tools,
but a lie is the handle which fits them all.

—Oliver Wendell Holmes, Sr.,
The Autocrat of the Breakfast Table

※ ※ ※

Almighty Lord,
According to your Word, I want to confess that
at times I have told lies to save face, to give a
certain impression, or to avoid doing something
I didn't want to do. Even though other people
may never discover I've been false, you see my sins,
heavenly Father. You know. I don't want to turn
to lying to get through my day, Lord. I know
you are a God of truth, and I want to be a child
who loves and walks in truth too. Cleanse me
from the unrighteousness of dishonesty, and help
me be committed to telling the truth, no matter
what it may cost me or how inconvenient it may
be. Help me be honest and true to you and your
Word. This I humbly pray. Amen.

※ ※ ※

Seek the Lord while He may be found;
    Call upon Him while He is near.
Let the wicked forsake his way,
    And the unrighteous man his
       thoughts;
    And let him return to the Lord, . . .
    For He will abundantly pardon.

ISAIAH 55:6–7 (NASB)

❋ ❋ ❋

Even as I look to you for forgiveness today,
Lord God, please grant me a strengthened
heart to follow through with true repentance.
Your forgiveness is given freely because of your
great love. Please fill me with a reciprocating
love that wants to draw near to you and
to your ways. Give me a heart that is not
at ease in sinful habits and paths, a heart that
returns to you and remains with you.

Let us ... approach the throne of grace
with boldness, so that we may receive
mercy and find grace to help in time
of need.

HEBREWS 4:16

※ ※ ※

*Help! I've been blindsided! I never thought
I'd find myself battling this sin, but here I am,
Lord, shocked and ashamed. It was my pride
that fueled my belief that I was "above" this sin,
and now I have fallen. How I need you! Indeed,
I need your forgiveness and your help to lead
me back to the right path. Even as I boldly
approach your throne of grace, I come to you
humbly. Please forgive me, Lord.*

※ ※ ※

Springing up from the soil
of our greatest transgressions forgiven
by God are the flowers of true humility
and gentle wisdom.

❈ ❈ ❈

Remember not the sins of my youth,
nor my transgressions: according to
thy mercy remember thou me for
thy goodness' sake, O Lord.

PSALM 25:7 (KJV)

❈ ❈ ❈

The ripeness of adolescence is prodigal
in pleasures, skittish, and in need of a bridle.

—PLUTARCH,
"THE EDUCATION OF CHILDREN," MORALIA

❈ ❈ ❈

Come now, and let us reason together, saith the Lord: though your sins be as scarlet, they shall be as white as snow; though they be red like crimson, they shall be as wool.

ISAIAH 1:18 (KJV)

Peace rules the day,
where reason rules the mind.

—WILLIAM COLLINS,
PERSIAN ECLOGUES

❋ ❋ ❋

It's wonderful to me that you are always extending your forgiveness to me. The world we live in seems always to be looking for reasons and ways to condemn and "crucify." Help me not "buy in" to the world's perspective. You call me to come to you and be reasonable, to see sin for what it is and to forsake it, to see your forgiveness for what it is and embrace it, and to see you for who you are and follow after you. I'm ready to come to you and accept the terms of this reasonable and gracious way of living, Lord. According to your mercy, I pray. Amen.

❋ ❋ ❋

CHAPTER 9

WHEN YOU'RE DEALING WITH DISAPPOINTMENT

Hope does not disappoint us,
because God's love has been
poured into our hearts
through the Holy Spirit that
has been given to us.

ROMANS 5:5

I have learned to be content with whatever I have. I know what it is to have little, and I know what it is to have plenty.... I can do all things through him who strengthens me.

PHILIPPIANS 4:11–13

※ ※ ※

Dear Lord, I thank you for the times of plenty that you have provided in the past. Now I turn to you in a time of need. Please strengthen me to deal with the current crisis. I'm not sure that I have the resources—physically or emotionally— to get through this, but I know you do. I rely on your power and your love to see me through.

※ ※ ※

He that is down needs fear no fall,
He that is low no pride.
He that is humble ever shall
Have God to be his guide.
I am content with what I have,
Little be it or much.

—JOHN BUNYAN, *PILGRIM'S PROGRESS*

※ ※ ※

I am confident of this, that the one
who began a good work among you
will bring it to completion by the day
of Jesus Christ.

PHILIPPIANS 1:6

※ ※ ※

Please be patient.
God is not finished with me yet.

—ANONYMOUS

Most merciful God, I realize that I come before you as a work in progress. Often I find myself in situations where I know the right thing to do, but I just don't do it. That's disappointing to me. I realize that I should have a better attitude about things and that I should trust you more and treat people better. But somehow you haven't given up on me. You keep reminding me of your support. You keep whispering your guidance. Thank you for this, and please keep working with me. Sometimes I'm a slow learner, but I want to learn.

✣ ✣ ✣

We know that all things work together
for good for those who love God,
who are called according to his purpose.

ROMANS 8:28

✣ ✣ ✣

Holy God, I don't get it. What is going on? I have tried to follow your ways, but lately that's becoming difficult. I don't know why you have allowed these disappointments to come my way. Have you stopped loving me? No. I know that can't be true, but then what's the answer? Can you really weave together these misfortunes into something "good"? I do love you, and I trust that you can make something good come out of this, but that would truly be a miracle, because it doesn't seem possible right now. Still, I'm going to try to hang on to my faith in you. You are much wiser than I am. So, please, work out your good purpose in my life.

❋ ❋ ❋

Eaten separately, the ingredients of
a chocolate cake might taste really awful.
But put together in the right recipe,
they're delicious—just like
the events of our lives.

❋ ❋ ❋

What then are we to say about these
things? If God is for us, who is against
us? He who did not withhold his own
Son, but gave him up for all of us, will
he not with him also give us everything
else?

ROMANS 8:31–32

❋ ❋ ❋

*God of hope and help, in my life I often feel
embattled. I struggle daily with people and
institutions and even machines. I don't know
why my existence has become so hard, but it has.
I long for peace. I long for comfort. I long for
things to go the way they're supposed to. It is
a great comfort to know that you are with me,
that you support me in my constant struggles.
Thank you for this, and please give me the
strength I need to keep going.*

❈ ❈ ❈

Be still my soul; the Lord is on your side.
Bear patiently the cross of grief or pain;
Leave to your God to order and provide;
In every change God faithful will remain.

—KATHARINA VON SCHLEGEL,
"BE STILL MY SOUL"

❈ ❈ ❈

For surely I know the plans I have for
you, says the Lord, plans for your
welfare and not for harm, to give you
a future with hope. Then when you
call upon me . . . I will hear you.

JEREMIAH 29:11–12

※ ※ ※

My brothers and sisters, whenever
you face trials of any kind, consider
it nothing but joy, because you know
that the testing of your faith produces
endurance; and let endurance have its
full effect, so that you may be mature
and complete, lacking in nothing.

JAMES 1:2–4

※ ※ ※

My Lord,

You know the deep hurt in my heart, but you promise healing. You know all about my worries and hurries, but you assure me of a better future. Often my vision is cast down. I put one foot in front of the other and plod through my fretful days, but you're opening the blinds, showing me a glorious panorama of a future filled with hope. Thank you for this inspiring vision. You have heard and answered prayers that I couldn't even put into words. You have lifted my spirit and my sight, and now I see the days ahead infused with your presence. I see you working mightily in me and through me to accomplish your purposes. The work you are doing in my life and in my character is beautiful to behold. Thank you again and again.

❊ ❊ ❊

We don't know what the future holds, but we
know who holds the future.

—Anonymous

※ ※ ※

My dear Lord,
I bow before you in humility, but isn't there
a better way? Yes, I want to be mature and
complete, but do I have to suffer so much? You
tell me to consider my trials "nothing but joy,"
and I want to, but is that realistic?All right, I
see that I'm growing through these tough times.
My faith is getting stronger as I learn to trust
you. And I see that I am better equipped to help
others because of what I've gone through, and
I'm glad for that, I really am. And yes, Lord, I
know that you've been with me through all my
disappointments, and I've been learning to rely
on you. I do thank you for helping me, but still . . .

Sorrow and silence are strong,
and patient endurance is godlike.

—HENRY WADSWORTH LONGFELLOW,
EVANGELINE

❈ ❈ ❈

Joseph said to them, "... Even though
you intended to do harm to me, God
intended it for good."

GENESIS 50:19–20

❈ ❈ ❈

God redeems us,
but he also redeems bad situations.
He has an uncanny knack for turning
the worst intentions into the best blessings.

❈ ❈ ❈

O God,

I have to tell you that people make me angry
sometimes. In fact, a lot of times. How can they
be so selfish, so ignorant, and so downright cruel?
I know you care for them too, but they must be
difficult to love, even for you. I have been deeply
hurt by some and just plain disappointed by
others, but I'm turning all these feelings over
to you. Is there any way you can turn these
injuries into something valuable?

❋ ❋ ❋

We also boast in our sufferings, knowing
that suffering produces endurance,
and endurance produces character,
and character produces hope.

Romans 5:3–4

❋ ❋ ❋

Creator God,
I see that you are still creating me. You are
patching the crevices and sanding the edges
and making me into something, somebody,
I'm not sure what. I can't say it's not painful,
but I trust that you know what you're doing.
Each challenge builds my character. Each
disappointment allows me to refocus my hope
in you, the only one I can really count on. Keep
doing your great work in me.

❋ ❋ ❋

Character isn't grown as much as it is honed,
sharpened against life's stones.

❋ ❋ ❋

"My grace is sufficient for you, for power is made perfect in weakness." . . . Therefore I am content with weaknesses, insults, hardships, persecutions, and calamities for the sake of Christ; for whenever I am weak, then I am strong.

2 CORINTHIANS 12:9–10

✼ ✼ ✼

When God wants to move a mountain,
he does not take a bar of iron,
but he takes a little worm.
The fact is, we have too much strength.
We are not weak enough.

—DWIGHT L. MOODY

✼ ✼ ✼

Lord Jesus,

I know all about weakness and disappointments. Just like the Apostle Paul, I want to do good, but I don't do it. I know what's wrong, and I find myself doing that. There are various character traits I might consider "thorns in my side." I constantly struggle with my own shortcomings and with disappointments in myself. I'm just weak. Why can't you just take away all that weakness and make me strong? Because you're the strong one, I guess. I may never understand this, but I accept it, and I rely on you for the strength to live each day.

※ ※ ※

Be strong and courageous; do not
be frightened or dismayed, for the
Lord your God is with you wherever
you go.

JOSHUA 1:9

※ ※ ※

*O Lord my God, as you know, there are things
in my life that are "dismaying" to me right now.
That's putting it mildly. Whatever strength or
courage I have must come from you. I cling to
the assurance that you will be with me. I can't
get through my disappointments on my own.
I need your comfort, your love, and your power.*

❊ ❊ ❊

Ye fearful saints fresh courage take,
The clouds ye so much dread
Are big with mercy, and shall break
In blessings on your head.

—WILLIAM COWPER,
"GOD MOVES IN A MYSTERIOUS WAY"

Why do you say…"My way is hidden
from the Lord, and my right is
disregarded by my God"? Have you
not known? Have you not heard?
The Lord is the everlasting God.

ISAIAH 40:27–28

❊ ❊ ❊

Before the hills in order stood,
or earth received her frame,
From everlasting, thou art God,
to endless years the same. . . .
O God our help in ages past,
our hope for years to come;
Be thou our guide while life shall last,
and our eternal home.

—ISAAC WATTS,
"O GOD, OUR HELP IN AGES PAST"

❊ ❊ ❊

Dear God,

Sometimes I feel really insignificant. You must have much more important things to deal with than my problems and disappointments. When things start to go wrong for me, I begin to worry that maybe you have forgotten about my concerns. I really wouldn't blame you. But then I read your Word again, and I'm touched by your promises. Even though you are the eternal, almighty Creator, you say you love me. You listen to my prayers. You want me to bring my disappointments before you. This is amazing to me and surprising. Why would you care about me? And yet you do. Thank you so much. You are my everlasting Lord.

❊ ❊ ❊

Do not fear, for I am with you, do
not be afraid, for I am your God; I
will strengthen you, I will help you,
I will uphold you with my victorious
right hand.

ISAIAH 41:10

※ ※ ※

Give to the winds thy fears;
hope and be undismayed.
God hears thy sighs and counts thy tears,
God shall lift up thy head.
Through waves and clouds and storms,
God gently clears thy way;
Wait thou God's time; so shall this night
soon end in joyous day.

—PAUL GERHARDT,
"GIVE TO THE WINDS THY FEARS"

※ ※ ※

Almighty God, you know the difficulties I've been facing lately, the deep sorrows and bitter disappointments I've gone through. It encourages me to know that you have been standing right with me through all of it. When I trust you, I feel my fear turning to faith. I feel your strength coursing through me when I need it most. When I begin to lose hope, you are there with a bright thought to keep my spirits up. When I feel like giving up, you empower me to keep going. You are my rock, my fortress, my champion, my savior. I thank you for all you have done for me.

❋ ❋ ❋

I have told you these things, so that in me you may have peace. In this world you will have trouble. But take heart! I have overcome the world.

JOHN 16:33 (NIV)

Prince of Peace,

I long for your peace. Turmoil is my constant companion. My troubles and disappointments have brought me anxiety and stress. It is somewhat comforting to know that this is no surprise to you. Trouble is part of this earthly life, but you have conquered it. I can expect that life won't be easy, but I must rely on you for survival. O Lord, bring that victory into my life. Let my attitude—every hour, every moment— reflect my complete confidence in you. I do believe that you have power over my troubles. Everything that's making my life difficult—you have already overcome it. So, in your power I'm moving forward. With your help I'll encounter whatever today brings and tomorrow too. Supported by your amazing strength, I will emerge victorious, and I'll give you all the glory.

※ ※ ※

Our attitude toward life's difficulties really
depends on what we're expecting.
If we anticipate unending bliss,
we'll be disappointed. But if we expect trouble,
we'll enjoy watching the ways God
gets us through it.

❋ ❋ ❋

And remember, I am with you always,
to the end of the age.

MATTHEW 28:20

❋ ❋ ❋

Dear Jesus,

Help me remember this when friends disappoint me. Remind me of your presence when it seems that everything else is going against me. When I face a challenge that seems too great for me, whisper that you are standing right behind me. When I worry that my own behavior has offended you, forgive me and hold me close to you. When I am distracted by my own worrying, help me focus on the truth that you are with me. When people misunderstand me and mistreat me, let me lean on you for support. When fears of the unknown make it difficult for me to move forward, gently lead me on. And when I draw my final breath, be there to carry me home.

※ ※ ※

Abide with me; fast falls the eventide;
The darkness deepens; Lord, with me abide.
When other helpers fail and comforts flee,
Help of the helpless, O abide with me.

—HENRY F. LYTE,
"ABIDE WITH ME"

※ ※ ※

With my voice I cry to the Lord;
  with my voice I make supplication
    to the Lord.
I pour out my complaint before him;
  I tell my trouble before him.
When my spirit is faint,
  you know my way.

PSALM 142:1–3

✳ ✳ ✳

You could assemble an impressive Hall of Fame
of people who bickered, argued, and haggled
with God: Abraham, Jacob, Moses, David,
Elijah, Jeremiah, Martha, Peter, Paul,
and so on. So don't be afraid to tell him how
you feel—honestly!

✳ ✳ ✳

You like tell-all biographies? Read the Bible.
You'll get the inside dirt on everyone.
That's what's amazing—and truly helpful—
about Scripture. All those "saints" were
just like us—faulty humans in touch
with a great God.

❊ ❊ ❊

*God of love and light and life, I thank you
today for a great gift you have given your people.
It wasn't enough to create us and set us on
a spinning world. You continued to guide us,
communicate with us, and tell us about
yourself—and about ourselves. So now I can
pick up a Bible and read the record of this
communication. That's a great blessing! In these
pages, you continually inspire me. Thank you,
dear Lord. Amen.*

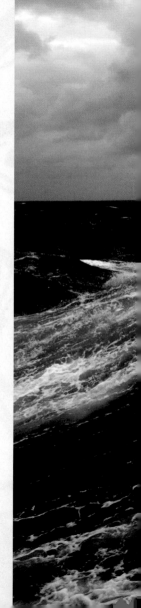

CHAPTER 10

WHEN YOU'RE RESPONDING TO A CRISIS

✳ ✳ ✳

Be not far from me,
for trouble is near;
For there is none to help.

PSALM 22:11 (NASB)

It's times like these that remind me, O Lord, that I'm not in control of my life and that I don't have all the answers. I feel stripped of my competency and my ability to work things out. This helplessness brings me near to a state of panic, but then you remind me that you are here for me. I can turn to you, call out to you, and put my trust in you. How long has it been since I have looked to you for help? I can be so independent and so self-sufficient sometimes. Thank you for this reminder that you are near and that I will never outlive my need for you. Please come walk me through this crisis and then help me continue walking by your side when I am beyond it.

※ ※ ※

In my distress I called upon the Lord;
to my God I called. From his temple
he heard my voice, and my cry came to
his ears.

2 SAMUEL 22:7

✦ ✦ ✦

A personal crisis is the strongest
truth serum against the tenacious lie that
we don't really need God's help.

✦ ✦ ✦

Though the Lord gave you adversity
for food and suffering for drink,
he will still be with you to teach you. . . .
Right behind you a voice will say,
"This is the way you should go."

ISAIAH 30:20–21 (NLT)

✦ ✦ ✦

I don't understand, Lord. Why? Why is this happening? Where are you? I don't even know which way to turn or what to do next. Did I do something wrong? Are you angry with me? Have you turned away from me? What do you mean by this? Please, I don't understand. I need you to take my hand and show me the way through this devastation. I need to know you're still with me.

The storm of circumstance may seem to
threaten the tiny vessel of my soul,
but Jesus is still on board with me,
and the echo of his command, "Peace!
Be still!" is able to calm not only
the storm around me but also
the disquiet of my own heart.

In the day of prosperity be joyful, and
in the day of adversity consider; God
has made the one as well as the other.

ECCLESIASTES 7:14

✻ ✻ ✻

O, how I miss the financial prosperity I was enjoying before these economic challenges came along. Dear Lord, I took so much for granted and imagined I was secure and that everything was all set up for the future. But truly there is no real security on earth, Lord, except in you. I see that now. Thank you for the good times, and thanks, too, for these lean times that bring me to a fuller understanding, reminding me that no matter what I lose in this life, I'll never lose your love.

❖ ❖ ❖

A . . . cruel disappointment, a loss of wealth, a loss of friends, seems at the moment unpaid loss, and unpayable. But the sure years reveal the deep remedial force that underlies all facts.

—RALPH WALDO EMERSON,
ESSAYS

David was greatly distressed;
for the people spoke of stoning him,
because all the people were bitter
in soul.... But David strengthened
himself in the Lord his God.

1 SAMUEL 30:6 (RSV)

❋ ❋ ❋

When written in Chinese,
the word "crisis" is composed of two
characters—one represents danger and
the other represents opportunity.

—JOHN F. KENNEDY

❋ ❋ ❋

Heavenly Father,
I feel so alone! It feels as though everyone has
turned against me or turned away from me
in some way. When things went south for me,
so did my friendships. I know people were
depending on me; I know they had certain
expectations, but I never anticipated this turn
of events. I don't know how to redeem myself,
Lord. I don't know how to turn things around.
Please be my support and my encouragement
and show me what to do next. I know you have
something in your plan for me in this crisis.
I'm so grateful that I can always count on
the faithfulness of your companionship and
steadfast love.

※ ※ ※

How the mighty have fallen in the
midst of the battle! Jonathan lies slain
upon your high places. I am distressed
for you, my brother Jonathan; greatly
beloved were you to me.

2 Samuel 1:25–26

※ ※ ※

We are never so defenseless
against suffering as when we love,
never so helplessly unhappy as when we have
lost our loved object or its love.

—Sigmund Freud,
Civilization and Its Discontents

※ ※ ※

Relieve the troubles of my heart,
and bring me out of my distress.

Psalm 25:17

※ ※ ※

The battlefields have claimed so many lives, almighty Father. One I have loved has been lost there. You know. This crisis of loss is too big for me to carry. I'm overcome with grief. It will never go away, but I am aware that time will bring a measure of relief from it. I cannot walk from here to there by myself. Please carry me until I can bear to walk beside you again. It might be awhile, but I'm assured of your tender strength that never fails. . . . How I look forward to the time when you will put an end to all wars and your perfect peace will reign forever!

❈ ❈ ❈

You see all that is pressing in around me, my Lord. It seems as if life itself is ganging up on me from all sides. At home and at work, in relationships and in finances, through physical and spiritual challenges I feel surrounded and unable to find any rest for my heart and mind. Please bring me relief! I lay all of these things before you and wait for your intervention and wisdom.

❋ ❋ ❋

While life's dark maze I tread
And griefs around me spread,
Be Thou my guide;
Bid darkness turn to day,
Wipe sorrow's tears away,
Nor let me ever stray
From Thee aside.

—RAY PALMER,
"MY FAITH LOOKS UP TO THEE"

Be gracious to me, O Lord,
for I am in distress; my eye wastes
away from grief, my soul and body also.

PSALM 31:9

※ ※ ※

*My soul feels shattered, heavenly Father. I didn't
know I could cry so many tears and still have
them come flowing all over again at just the
thought of what has happened. My appetite for
life is gone. I am like a shadow moving among
the people around me who are enjoying life. I
feel so cut off from them, as if I'm in another
kind of reality. We're in the same physical world,
but I find no common ground for relating to
others in it. Please help me. I don't even know
what to ask for except for your mercy and grace
to break through to me.*

※ ※ ※

Expectation unraveled
Reality in a heap
At my standstill feet.
Let my heart alone awhile
To gather and hold
Its grief.

—Christine A. Dallman

※ ※ ※

Let everyone who is godly pray to you
while you may be found; surely when
the mighty waters rise, they will not
reach him. You are my hiding place;
you will protect me from trouble and
surround me with songs of deliverance.

Psalm 32:6–7 (NIV)

※ ※ ※

Almighty Father,

In the past I might have thought that what is taught in Scripture meant that I was exempt from any kind of trouble as long as I trusted in you. But I'm coming to understand, as one who lives in a fallen world with trouble all around me, that I'm bound to face adversity, trouble, and crises. You know, Lord, that people have cheated and abused, hurt and disillusioned me over and over again. But the mighty waters of bitterness and hatred have not overcome me because, in your love and forgiveness, I find refuge from them. Please help me once again as I seek the refuge of your goodness in this fallen and often troublesome world.

❊ ❊ ❊

When I wanted to take refuge from
the adversity around me, I found that
I needed refuge from myself as well.
Of course, God is the only one who provides
that particular kind of protection.

※ ※ ※

I will sing aloud of your steadfast love
in the morning. For you have been
a fortress for me and a refuge in the
day of my distress. O my strength,
I will sing praises to you.

PSALM 59:16–17

※ ※ ※

Dear Lord,

Who could possibly sing in the middle of a crisis?
Only those who know for certain they are safe
in your love. Only those who are comforted by
the knowledge of your faithfulness. O! Let me
be one who sings today because of who you are,
no matter what crisis I'm going through. Put
a joyful song in my soul today. I pray in Jesus'
name. Amen.

❋ ❋ ❋

A mighty fortress is our God,
A bulwark never failing;
Our helper, He amid the flood
Of mortal ills prevailing.

—MARTIN LUTHER,
"A MIGHTY FORTRESS IS OUR GOD"

❋ ❋ ❋

I walk before the Lord in the land
of the living. I kept my faith,
even when I said, "I am greatly
afflicted."

PSALM 116:9–10

※ ※ ※

*Grant me the kind of faith that can turn my face
forward to the future, even in the middle of all
that is transpiring in my life right now. I declare
my trust in you, Lord God. Life is fleeting, but I
belong to eternity. Help me keep my eyes on the
best that is yet to come.*

※ ※ ※

I have often been downcast,
but never in despair.... In my diary I treat
all the privations as amusing.... My start has
been so very full of interest, and that is the sole
reason why I have to laugh at the humorous
side of the most dangerous moments.

—ANNE FRANK,
THE DIARY OF A YOUNG GIRL

❈ ❈ ❈

Out of my distress I called on
the Lord; the Lord answered me
and set me free.

PSALM 118:5 (RSV)

❈ ❈ ❈

Man's extremity is God's opportunity.

—JOHN FLAVEL

❈ ❈ ❈

I'm trapped! There's no way out of this! Help me, Lord! I feel like a bird in a snare, one who will be put in a cage for the rest of its life! Show me the way to freedom—the true freedom that comes from your answers, not the temporary but fleeting freedom of my own solutions. I'm in your hands.

❈ ❈ ❈

You have been a refuge to the poor,
a refuge to the needy in their distress,
a shelter from the rainstorm and
a shade from the heat.

ISAIAH 25:4

❈ ❈ ❈

Great crises produce great men and great
deeds of courage.

—JOHN F. KENNEDY,
PROFILES IN COURAGE

Dear heavenly Father,

The month-to-month battle of meeting my temporal needs feels like an ongoing crisis. There never seems to be enough money coming in to cover what money is going out. Somehow you carry me through, but I work so hard only to barely scrape by. And I have to admit, I feel oppressed by those for whom I work; I work so hard, and yet, I don't feel valued or adequately compensated for what I do. I'm worn out by the stress of it all. I'm tired of working and not being able to have anything left over for maintaining the household and the car and other pressing needs. Please! Come bring me relief from the intensity of this continual stress. Please be my shade from the heat of the daily grind. Grant me your strength and deliverance.

❊ ❊ ❊

This is my Father's world
Oh, let me ne'er forget
That though the wrong seems oft so strong,
God is the ruler yet.

—MALTHIE D. BABCOCK,
"THIS IS MY FATHER'S WORLD"

❈ ❈ ❈

That's why I take pleasure in my
weaknesses, and in the insults,
hardships, persecutions, and troubles
that I suffer for Christ. For when I
am weak, then I am strong.

2 CORINTHIANS 12:10 (NLT)

❈ ❈ ❈

Dear Lord,

Teach me to say with the Apostle Paul that the crises in my life are occasions for acknowledging my own weakness as I embrace your perfect strength. Please remind me today, as I navigate the current circumstances, that this is an opportunity for me to do just that. Let the power of this adversity so shape my character that I become a person of greater courage because I have learned to lean into you and be carried along in your powerful love.

❈ ❈ ❈

We also exult in our tribulations, knowing that tribulation brings about perseverance; and perseverance, proven character; and proven character, hope.

ROMANS 5:3–4 (NASB)

I can't say yet that I'm "exulting" in my trials right now, Lord. But I know there will come a day when I will see what they have brought about in my life, and I'll be grateful. So I ask that you would help me begin to thank you now, since I know you are faithfully sculpting me through these current tribulations and hard times, making me into the person of faith I long to become.

※ ※ ※

Every man deems that he has precisely the trials...which are the hardest of all others for him to bear; but they are so, simply because they are the very ones he most needs.

—LYDIA M. CHILD

※ ※ ※

For just as the sufferings of Christ
are abundant for us, so also our
consolation is abundant through
Christ.

2 CORINTHIANS 1:5

※ ※ ※

I consider that the sufferings of this
present time are not worth comparing
with the glory about to be revealed
to us.

ROMANS 8:18

※ ※ ※

Misfortune is never mournful to the soul
that accepts it; for such do always see
that every cloud is an angel's face.

—LYDIA M. CHILD

※ ※ ※

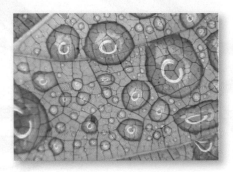

Dear Lord,

Let the weight of my circumstances today remind me of a time that is yet to come, when you will wipe every tear from my eyes and usher me into an eternal home with you. I know that you do not intend that I escape reality in such thoughts. But your promises do make a way for me to walk through the present crisis with hope and courage, knowing that this is not a stopping point in my life, but a mere via point on my way to my true destination. In Jesus' name, I pray. Amen.

✳ ✳ ✳

CHAPTER 11

WHEN YOU'RE
EXPERIENCING
SORROW

✻ ✻ ✻

Can we find a friend so faithful
Who will all our sorrows share?
Jesus knows our every weakness;
Take it to the Lord in prayer.

—JOSEPH M. SCRIVEN,
"WHAT A FRIEND WE HAVE IN JESUS"

Lord! O, Lord!

This heartache has swallowed me whole. I can't find a place where I am ever apart from it. I can't imagine ever not feeling this way, and I can't remember what it was like to be carefree. I feel so helpless, and I don't know where to find the will to take the next step. Somehow I do keep going, but it's as if I'm sleepwalking, and I don't know what will happen if I come out of this half-haze. I know I need you more than ever, but I'm struggling to lift my heart to you. I just need you to be here. I need you to hold me together. I need you to hold me. Be my comfort, please, Lord. Somehow, soothe this soul of mine.

❈ ❈ ❈

O my Comforter in sorrow,
my heart is faint within me.

JEREMIAH 8:18 (NIV)

There are no shortcuts through grief,
only a path, along which our Lord himself
has walked and will walk with us
with his gentle strength.

※ ※ ※

Blessed are those who mourn,
for they will be comforted.

MATTHEW 5:4

※ ※ ※

Even as my heart is full of sorrow, heavenly Father, thank you for the blessing of your comfort. I admit, sometimes I don't even realize you've come with your gentle touch until the moment passes. But I'm grateful for each bit of comfort you bring. Those blessed distractions— a hummingbird at the feeder, my pet's needs and affections, and a visit or phone call from a friend—these things give me a break from the ever-encroaching sadness. And the reasons to keep going—people you've given me to love, skills and abilities I have to contribute to help others, and the sense of a future (however vague it might seem right now)—all remind me that grief is not all there is to life. Help me not reject these kindnesses from your hand but allow them to become a part of my healing.

※ ※ ※

Those who know best how to comfort
a sorrowing friend have themselves needed
comfort along the way.

※ ※ ※

My soul melts away for sorrow;
strengthen me according to your word.

PSALM 119:28

※ ※ ※

Lord God,
I appreciate the way the Bible is honest about
the realities of sorrow. I find comfort especially
in the psalms, where the hurting soul is not
hidden and yet the call to trust is always there.
As I look to your Word, please help me find the
encouragement you know I need.

※ ※ ※

Opening the Bible in times of sorrow is
like removing the lid from a deep well during
a drought to draw out life-sustaining water.

He was despised and rejected by men,
a man of sorrows, and familiar with
suffering.... Surely he took up our
infirmities and carried our sorrows...
and by his wounds we are healed.

ISAIAH 53:3–5 (NIV)

Dear Jesus,

In your suffering, you have come alongside me.
In your grief, I see that you fully understand
mine. In your sacrifice, I realize that you care
and have given your all for me. And yet, I still
struggle to understand why you've allowed this
great sorrow in my life. Where my pain threatens
my trust in you, please keep me from doubt
and resentment. Let the reminder of you as my
sympathetic Savior renew my faith in your love
and good purposes for my life.

❋ ❋ ❋

Though Satan should buffet,
though trials should come
Let this blest assurance control,
That Christ has regarded my helpless estate,
And hath shed his own blood for my soul.

—HORATIO G. SPAFFORD,
"IT IS WELL WITH MY SOUL"

Let your steadfast love become my
comfort
according to your promise....
Let your mercy come to me, that I
may live.

PSALM 119:76–77

❋ ❋ ❋

Each day your mercy comes to me in more ways than I can name in one prayer. The mercy of your being here with me buffers the powerful sorrow that rushes in when I wake in the morning. The mercy of your forgiveness and compassion soothes my aching mind and conscience. The mercy of your goodness—all the practical ways you are caring for me—helps me through the day. The mercy of good memories and hope for the future give me courage to walk on. I desperately need your mercy, and you give it to me so freely.

As the raindrops of mercy began to fall softly
from heaven, I couldn't feel them at first.
Before long, however, I was soaked through
with the warm gentleness of divine love.

❈ ❈ ❈

To everything there is a season, a time
for every purpose under heaven:
A time to be born, and a time to die;
. . . a time to weep, and a time to laugh.

ECCLESIASTES 3:1–2, 4 (NKJV)

❈ ❈ ❈

Here let me wait with patience,
Wait till the night is o'er,
Wait till I see the morning
Break on the golden shore.

—FANNY J. CROSBY,
"SAFE IN THE ARMS OF JESUS"

I wasn't ready for this loss, Lord. I wasn't prepared for how much this would hurt. And even though I have entrusted my loved ones to you, knowing they belong to you, this parting is deeply painful. I realize that the passing of your children from this earth and into your heaven is a cause for rejoicing, but those of us who are left waiting here can't help but weep. How we miss them! We wait for the day when you'll turn all our mourning into laughter. Until then, we seek your comfort. I seek your comfort and need you to hold me close as I mourn in the shadowy valley of death.

God himself will be with them and
be their God. He will wipe every tear
from their eyes. There will be no more
death or mourning or crying or pain,
for the old order of things has passed
away.

REVELATION 21:3–4 (NIV)

※ ※ ※

Heavenly Father,
I believe that one day, you'll make everything
new. I hold on to that hope while I'm slogging
through this earthly mire of sorrow, while my
tears flow and my heart breaks. I believe, not as
though in a fairy tale that might come true, but
as in a promise made by the One who has never
lied nor failed. I believe in you, in your promise,
and in your love for me. Preserve me in that love,
I pray. Amen.

Faith is to believe what you do not yet see;
the reward for this faith is to see
what you believe.

—St. Augustine, *Sermons*, 43

❈ ❈ ❈

Even in laughter the heart may sorrow,
and the end of mirth may be grief.

Proverbs 14:13 (NKJV)

❈ ❈ ❈

So often I have to put on a brave face, Lord,
a smile just to get through an encounter or
situation, but you see my heart. What would
I do without you? How would I get through if
I didn't have you as my place of refuge, the one
who supports me from within? I'm leaning
entirely on you even though no one else may
know how much I'm struggling.

Sometimes even to live is an act of courage.

—SENECA,
LETTERS TO LUCILIUS

❋ ❋ ❋

[The Lord] has sent me to bind up the
brokenhearted, . . . to bestow…the oil
of gladness instead of mourning, and
a garment of praise instead of a spirit
of despair.

ISAIAH 61:1, 3 (NIV)

❋ ❋ ❋

Heavenly Father,
I'm so glad your compassion isn't passive.
You sent Jesus to open the way to healing and
wholeness for me. I long for my broken heart to
be bandaged, my mourning to melt into gladness,
and my despair to become praise … but only in
your way, in your time, and as you will. I'm in
your hands, Lord, the only hands that can bring
the true healing I need.

※ ※ ※

When our ill-fitting garments of grief
are worn out, it is Jesus who comes to clothe
us in new, tailor-made garments of gladness.

※ ※ ※

Very truly, I tell you, you will weep
and mourn, . . . you will have pain, but
your pain will turn into joy.

JOHN 16:20

Dear Jesus,

You told your disciples that there would be a time of grieving for them, but you didn't leave them without hope. You told them that they'd shed their grief and be reborn into joy. O! How I long to find joy again, to have my soul's burdens roll off, and to feel as if I could take flight, to have the sunshine lift my spirits like it used to, and to look forward to things I once enjoyed doing. How long will it be, Lord? I wonder. If I could just shake myself free, I would. But I know I need your resurrection power to bring new life, your healing Spirit to blow through my broken spirit. I look forward to the day when I will look back on my grief from a heart full of joy. In your precious and holy name, I pray.

※ ※ ※

God's timing, based on his eternal perspective,
bids our faith wait patiently for joy's
triumphant arrival.

✴ ✴ ✴

We do not want you to…grieve like
[those], who have no hope. We believe
that Jesus died and rose again and so
we believe that God will bring with
Jesus those who have fallen asleep
in him.

1 Thessalonians 4:13–14 (NIV)

✴ ✴ ✴

But lo! There breaks a yet more glorious day;
The saints triumphant rise in bright array;
The King of glory passes on His way.
Alleluia! Alleluia!

—William W. How,
"For All the Saints"

Fill me with the hope of what is to come,
heavenly Father, so that my grief is not the kind
that's permanent or despairing. You've provided
the gift of eternal life. All who put their trust in
you will live together again with you one day.
Grant me the faith to believe that just as you've
promised, so it will be.

❋ ❋ ❋

You, O God, do see trouble and grief;
you consider it to take it in hand.
The victim commits himself to you;
you are the helper of the fatherless.

PSALM 10:14 (NIV)

❋ ❋ ❋

I only ask to be free.
The butterflies are free.

—CHARLES DICKENS,
BLEAK HOUSE

Why? Why, Lord?
Why did you allow me to be victimized when
I was so helpless? The sorrow it has caused is
still with me. Yet your Word says that you see
and consider and even take into hand this pain
I carry. I've carried it so long that I don't really
know how to lay it down. But I believe you
can show me and that you can lift it from my
shoulders and cast it away. Would you? Show
me what I need to do, step by step, to follow you
into freedom. God of love, be my helper. Be my
heavenly Father. Become my joy. In Jesus' name,
I pray. Amen.

There is no fruit which is not bitter
before it is ripe.

—PUBLILIUS SYRUS,
MORAL SAYINGS

For a little while you may have had
to suffer grief in all kinds of trials.
These have come so that your faith…
may be proved genuine and may result
in praise, glory and honor when Jesus
Christ is revealed.

1 PETER 1:6–7 (NIV)

Heavenly Father,
Don't let this sorrow be in vain. Even when I
question why, cause my faith to grow strong and
true. Even as I suffer and grieve, help me lift my
eyes to see the bigger picture of your purposes
and plan. Prepare me for the day when I'll
move beyond this temporary situation into a
permanent, eternal joy.

✵ ✵ ✵

My flesh and my heart may fail, but
God is the strength of my heart and
my portion forever.

PSALM 73:26

✵ ✵ ✵

For this relief much thanks: 'tis bitter cold,
And I am sick at heart.

—SHAKESPEARE, *HAMLET*

When the debilitating waves of sorrow crash over me, heavenly Father, sweeping me away in their powerful current, rescue me from being carried out to sea—out to the sea of despair and unbelief. Be my lifeguard, my rescue ship, my anchor—everything that brings salvation, safety, and stability, as only you can bring them, please.

※ ※ ※

Weeping may linger for the night,
but joy comes with the morning.

PSALM 30:5

❊ ❊ ❊

Dear Lord,
I keep waiting for the morning, for the hints on
the horizon of daybreak. But the sky is still dark,
and it feels as though I've been forever in the
night. Please grant me the strength to look up
and find the blessing of starlight as I endure
until dawn. As I weep, you wait with me, I
know. Thank you for remaining with me, for
encouraging me, and for filling me with hope.
And you will be here to rejoice with me in the
morning. Together we'll watch the sunrise.

❊ ❊ ❊

As one by one thy hopes depart,
Be resolute and calm.
O fear not in a world like this,
And thou shalt know ere long,
Know how sublime a thing it is
To suffer and be strong.

—HENRY WADSWORTH LONGFELLOW,
"THE LIGHT OF STARS"

❊ ❊ ❊

The length of our days is . . .
but trouble and sorrow,
for [the years] quickly pass,
and we fly away. . . .
Teach us to number our days . . .
that we may gain a heart of wisdom.

PSALM 90:10, 12 (NIV)

❊ ❊ ❊

Wisdom is ofttimes nearer when we stoop
Than when we soar.

—WILLIAM WORDSWORTH,
THE EXCURSION

❈ ❈ ❈

Thank you for the wisdom and maturity that have come into my life through sorrow, O Lord. While I would not have asked for this pain to enter my life, I can see some of your good purposes for permitting it. Please grant me the ability to turn and help others who are struggling with similar grief. Help me extend empathy and support. Help me remember how I felt. And help me extend the patience and gentleness I, too, needed when I was engulfed in my heartache. Let me be an extension of your tender mercies to the hurting ones around me. In Jesus' name, I pray. Amen.

❋ ❋ ❋

CHAPTER 12

WHEN YOU'RE
BATTLING
DEPRESSION

*Weeping may linger
for the night,
but joy comes with
the morning.*

PSALM 30:5

A new heart I will give you, and a new
spirit I will put within you; and I will
remove from your body the heart of
stone and give you a heart of flesh.

EZEKIEL 36:26

※ ※ ※

Dear Lord,
Sometimes I feel as if my heart is made of stone.
Nothing seems to sink in. I find myself incapable
of loving, caring, and feeling. I need a new start,
Lord, a new heart. You're the one who can make
that happen. Work a miracle of resurrection
in me, a miracle of regeneration, and help me
love once more. I can't remain who I am. I need
you to change me.

※ ※ ※

There is not one blade of grass,
there is no color in this world
that is not intended
to make us rejoice.

—JOHN CALVIN

❈ ❈ ❈

Go your way…
for this day is holy to our Lord;
and do not be grieved,
for the joy of the Lord is your strength.

NEHEMIAH 8:10

❈ ❈ ❈

God is enjoying himself and
he expects us to join him.

—MEISTER ECKHART

❈ ❈ ❈

Holy God,

I have sat idle through too many worship services.
I have watched passively while everyone else was
rejoicing and praising. Somehow, I haven't felt the
fire. I guess I've been dwelling on my own woes.
But let me declare this day as "holy to the Lord."
This is the day I put aside my grief. This is the
moment I dare to take part in your joy. Lord,
let me find strength in you. Let me burst out
of my doldrums and step out with power as I
experience the blessing of knowing you.

※ ※ ※

When you pass through the waters,
    I will be with you;
and through the rivers, they shall not
    overwhelm you;
when you walk through fire you shall
    not be burned,
and the flame shall not consume you.

ISAIAH 43:2

※ ※ ※

I have been feeling overwhelmed, heavenly Father, by things going on in my life and by my reactions to them. Fear and anxiety sap my energy. I'm not sure what to do next. Can you help me? Guide me through these difficult situations, and give me strength to move forward. More than anything, just be with me. Keep assuring me of your presence.

※ ※ ※

If you tell your troubles to God,
you put them into the grave;
if you roll your burden somewhere else,
it will roll back again.

—Charles Haddon Spurgeon

❈ ❈ ❈

If anyone is in Christ,
there is a new creation:
everything old has passed away;
see, everything has become new!

2 Corinthians 5:17

❈ ❈ ❈

God creates out of nothing.
So until someone is nothing,
God can make nothing out of him.

—Martin Luther

❈ ❈ ❈

Gracious God,

There are many things in my past I'm not proud of. You know the multitude of sins and bad decisions I've accumulated. Many times I insisted on going my own way rather than following you. I recognize that much of my current stress stems from those times. But can we turn the page on that? Can you really erase those sins and start something new in my life? I trust you to accomplish that massive reclamation project. I know I can't do it myself, but you have the power. Let the past truly pass away, and let the future blossom into new life.

O hope of every contrite heart,
O joy of all the meek,
To those who fall, how kind thou art!
How good to those who seek!

—Attributed to Bernard of Clairvaux,
"Jesus the Very Thought of Thee"

※ ※ ※

To him who is able to keep you from
falling, and to make you stand without
blemish in the presence of his glory
with rejoicing, to the only God our
Savior…be glory, majesty, power, and
authority.

Jude 24–25

※ ※ ※

One help for depression: Realize that everyone
else is just as needy as you are.

※ ※ ※

My Savior,

I find myself falling into depression. I have watched parts of my life collapse before my eyes—relationships, work, dreams—and now my emotions are running wild. One day I'm weepy, the next day I'm as cold as stone. I don't know what's going on with me, but I know I need help. Your help. If you are really able to pull me out of this depression, please act now to do that. I have nothing to offer you in return, except my enduring gratitude. For whatever miracle you perform in my life, I will give you all the glory.

※ ※ ※

See what love the Father has given us, that we should be called children of God.

1 JOHN 3:1

※ ※ ※

I will greatly rejoice in the Lord,
my whole being shall exult in my God;
for he has clothed me with the
garments of salvation, he has covered
me with the robe of righteousness.

ISAIAH 61:10

※ ※ ※

*I forget this too often, heavenly Father. I am
your child. That gives me some hope when I'm
feeling down, like right now. I am your child.
That means you love me, and you keep loving me
even when I disappoint you. That's comforting.
I guess there's also comfort in the fact that,
like a child, I'm still growing. I'm still learning.
You are molding me into something better. I am
your child. Thank you, Father, for that simple
truth.*

※ ※ ※

Almighty God,

Sometimes I feel as though I'm wearing ripped-up jeans at a formal banquet. Everyone else looks so perfect in their suits and gowns, and I'm a slob. Everyone else has the perfect words to say, but I'm tongue-tied. I look around at other people, and they're serving you powerfully, effectively, and righteously, while I struggle to do the simplest act of devotion. What's wrong with me? I begin to take some comfort in those Bible verses that talk about you as a fashion designer—after all, you have clothed me in the garments of salvation. No matter how inappropriately I dress, you can find a way to adorn me in the finest apparel. Even though I have made a mess of my life, you can make me presentable again.

※ ※ ※

As the hand is made for holding and the eye for
seeing, thou hast fashioned me for joy.
Share with me the vision that shall find
it everywhere.

—Gaelic prayer

✳ ✳ ✳

O taste and see that the Lord is good;
happy are those who take refuge
in him.

Psalm 34:8

✳ ✳ ✳

Dear Lord,

I've been thinking about the tastes I love—the temptation of my favorite dessert, the aroma wafting from the cup I drink each morning, and the signature dish of the restaurant I frequent. I can think of you like that, too, as I "taste" your goodness. But one of the problems of my bouts with depression is that I lose my sense of taste. When I'm feeling down, that dessert doesn't carry the same satisfaction. All my senses get dulled. Enjoyment seems distant. Lord, I ask you to wake me from my depression and wake up those senses, and please start with my sensation of your presence. Be near me, and let me tingle with the sense of your nearness. I want to taste your goodness as fully as possible.

❊ ❊ ❊

The best things are nearest:
breath in your nostrils, light in your eyes,
flowers at your feet, duties at your hand,
the path of God just before you.

—ROBERT LOUIS STEVENSON

✕ ✕ ✕

Comfort me, dear Lord. I sorely need your reassuring words, because I have suffered a great loss and feel a deep depression coming over me. Instead, I want to feel your warm embrace, because I am in such mourning. Whisper to me of your love. Describe for me a brighter future. Let me know that you are with me. Bless me with your comfort.

✕ ✕ ✕

Blessed are those who mourn,
for they will be comforted.

MATTHEW 5:4

❊ ❊ ❊

The supreme happiness of life is
the conviction that we are loved.

—VICTOR HUGO

❊ ❊ ❊

Since we are justified by faith,
we have peace with God through
our Lord Jesus Christ, . . . and we
boast in our hope of sharing the
glory of God.

ROMANS 5:1–2

❊ ❊ ❊

Lord Jesus,

I've been feeling distant from you lately, and I know it's my fault that I am so depressed about my estrangement from you. Too often I have strayed into behavior you don't like. Instead of standing up to temptation, I buckle under. As a result, I feel weak, dirty, embarrassed, and unworthy to be in your presence. And maybe those feelings have kept me from coming back to you. It's hard for me to address you now, but I know it's the only way I'll find anything resembling joy in my life. Can you restore this relationship to something like what it used to be? That's what I want, Lord, and I humbly beg for your forgiveness. Please bring my spirit back to life.

※ ※ ※

Jesus, joy of our desiring, holy wisdom,
love most bright,
Drawn by thee, our souls aspiring soar
to uncreated light....
Through the way where hope is guiding,
hark, what peaceful music rings,
Where the flock, in thee confiding,
drink of joy from deathless springs.

—MARTIN JANUS,
"JESUS, JOY OF OUR DESIRING"

✤ ✤ ✤

You rejoice, even if now for a
little while you have had to suffer
various trials, so that the genuineness
of your faith . . . may be found to result
in praise and glory and honor.

1 PETER 1:6–7

✤ ✤ ✤

"This is a test. This is only a test." That's what I keep telling myself, Lord, but it still feels awful. You have allowed the circumstances of my life to become extremely difficult, and I have tried to slog through in faith, but I'm afraid I've lost my joy and have become depressed. I used to find pleasure in worshipping you, but lately it's just something I'm supposed to do. Please, Lord, restore the joy I had before. Let's get this trial over with, so we can move quickly into "praise, glory, and honor." I'm not sure I have the strength to last much longer.

✳ ✳ ✳

No pain, no palm; no thorns, no throne;
no gall, no glory; no cross, no crown.

—WILLIAM PENN

✳ ✳ ✳

This one thing I do: forgetting what
lies behind and straining forward
to what lies ahead, I press on toward
the goal for the prize of the heavenly
call of God in Christ Jesus.

PHILIPPIANS 3:13–14

Too long now I've been stuck in the past. Lord, you know the regrets I have, the losses I've sustained, the pain I've felt. These memories have paralyzed me, sapping my strength and shutting down my heart. But now it's time to move forward. This scares me, Lord. The future is uncertain at best. How can I be sure I won't just reopen the old wounds? I guess that's where faith comes in. Lord, I don't have much faith to offer, just a mustard seed, but I count on you to make it grow. Lead me forward. Lift my sights. Give me the strength to press on toward the goal. Help me win that prize.

※ ※ ※

You don't win the Indy 500 by driving in reverse. And you don't serve God effectively by gazing at your past.

※ ※ ※

You show me the path of life.
In your presence there is fullness
  of joy;
in your right hand are pleasures
  forevermore.

PSALM 16:11

※ ※ ※

Great God,
I ask you to show me this path of life. Lead me
step by step in the kind of life you want for me.
Help me steer clear of the activities that kill the
spirit or deaden the soul. Reanimate my numb
emotions, deliver me from dark depression,
and let me rediscover the joy of your presence.

Joyful, joyful, we adore thee,
God of glory, Lord of love.
Hearts unfold like flowers before thee,
opening to the sun above.
Melt the clouds of sin and sadness,
drive the dark of doubt away.
Giver of immortal gladness,
fill us with the light of day!

—Henry van Dyke,
"Joyful, Joyful, We Adore Thee"

✳ ✳ ✳

Why are you cast down, O my soul,
and why are you disquieted within
me? Hope in God; for I shall again
praise him, my help and my God.

Psalm 42:5–6

✳ ✳ ✳

God of hope,
I'm not sure how I sank this far into depression.
Sorrow struck and robbed me of all laughter.
I stopped seeing your signature written on the
world around me. I began to fear, to sulk, and to
think only of my own protection. At first it was
just a bad mood, but that became a sour spirit
and dragged on into chronic bitterness. Why
is my soul cast down? I don't even remember
now.... But in this moment I hear the faint lilt of
a song. Praise is drifting into my consciousness,
reminding me that you are a God who helps
people like me. You raise up the fallen, you
comfort the sorrowful, and you bring the dead
back to life. I sense a spark of hope within my
heart. Can you fan that into a radiant flame?

※ ※ ※

There are times when we're going to feel depressed, vindictive, and anxious. The question is: What happens to those feelings when God enters the picture? The Bible teaches us how to invite God into our emotions.

※ ※ ※

Come to me, all you that are weary
and are carrying heavy burdens,
and I will give you rest.

MATTHEW 11:28

※ ※ ※

Jesus, the very thought of thee
with sweetness fills my breast.
But sweeter far thy face to see,
and in thy presence rest.

—ATTRIBUTED TO BERNARD OF CLAIRVAUX,
"JESUS, THE VERY THOUGHT OF THEE"

※ ※ ※

I'm coming to you now with heavy burdens, Lord Jesus. You know the troubles I've been through. You understand the toll they've taken on my heart. I'm finding it hard to trust anyone these days, but I'm going to trust you. I'm sick and tired of feeling depressed. My misfortunes have brought me a deep weariness of heart that only you can cure. So I'm coming to you for rest. Take this burden off my back. Salve my soul. Please give me your peace.

✸ ✸ ✸

I waited patiently for the Lord;
he inclined to me and heard my cry.
He drew me up from the desolate
pit....He put a new song in my mouth.

PSALM 40:1–3

✸ ✸ ✸

We must wait for God,
long, meekly, in the wind and wet,
in the thunder and lightning,
in the cold and dark. Wait, and he will come.
He never comes to those who do not wait.

—Frederick William Faber

※ ※ ※

Patience is a marvelous virtue, dear Lord, but it takes so long to get it! I feel as if I've been waiting forever to burst out of these doldrums, crying out to you for some sort of restoration. But I'll wait longer, because I believe that you will answer. Someday you will lift me up into a life that sparkles, a life that touches others with vibrant love. That's hard to imagine now, but I believe it's coming. Someday you will give me a new song to sing, a song that acknowledges that the hard times are past and looks ahead to a glorious future. I trust that you will hear my cry and deliver me, and so I'll wait a little longer. In Jesus' name, I pray. Amen.

※ ※ ※

CHAPTER 13

WHEN YOU'RE QUESTIONING YOUR FAITH

✹ ✹ ✹

All I have seen
teaches me to trust
the Creator
for all I have not seen.

—RALPH WALDO EMERSON

Dear Lord,

Where are you? For some reason you don't feel as close to me as you used to. There was a time when I sensed your presence in everything I did: in my home, in my work, and in my relationships. Recent events, however, have made me wonder if you still care about me. I know times are tough for everyone, but I always expected that you'd help me through my problems. Now I plod through my life without you. Even church seems like a charade. Did I do something wrong? Or are you testing me in some way? Whatever the issue is, let's clear it up. I miss you. I want you back in my life. Please let me know you're here with me.

※ ※ ※

"If you feel far from God, guess who moved?"
That makes a clever bumper sticker,
but it's not always true. God *does* step back
from us sometimes, just to give us
the experience of seeking him.

❊ ❊ ❊

For my thoughts are not your
 thoughts,
nor are your ways my ways, says
 the Lord.
For as the heavens are higher than
 the earth,
so are my ways higher than your ways
and my thoughts than your thoughts.

ISAIAH 55:8–9

❊ ❊ ❊

Seek the Lord while he may be found,
call upon him while he is near.

ISAIAH 55:6

※ ※ ※

Dear God,
Maker of heaven and earth, I bow down before
you, but I'm not always sure why. I honor you
as the Lord of all, but I don't really understand
what you're doing. I see people suffering left and
right—good people, folks who deserve better.
Meanwhile, the fat cats who caused the whole
mess are flying high, untouched by our misery.
Is this any way to run a world? I don't get it.
I don't mean to be disrespectful, I really don't,
but I have to wonder how you can let things
go on like this.

※ ※ ※

Everyone knows the theme of the Book of Job:
"Why do bad things happen to good people?"
The odd thing is that God never really answers
the question. He basically says,
"I'm God and you're not."

Jesus said to him, ". . . All things can be
done for the one who believes."
Immediately the father of the child
cried out, "I believe; help my unbelief!"

MARK 9:23–24

Dear Jesus,
I find myself at the intersection of faith and
doubt. I do believe in you, but it's not always easy.
I have a lot of questions, a lot of problems, and
not very many answers. When I was younger,
I had a lot of confidence, but not so much now.
Help me, Lord Jesus, in my unbelief. Fan the
flickering flame of my faith.

❈ ❈ ❈

I am not ashamed, for I know the one
in whom I have put my trust, and I am
sure that he is able to guard until that
day what I have entrusted to him.

2 TIMOTHY 1:12

❈ ❈ ❈

Faith embraces many truths which seem to
contradict one another.

—BLAISE PASCAL

There lies more faith in honest doubt,
believe me, than in half the creeds.

—ALFRED LORD TENNYSON,
IN MEMORIAM

⁂ ⁂ ⁂

Beloved Lord,

*There are many things I don't know. People ask
me questions about you that I can't answer.
When scientific discussions or philosophical
debates start up, I don't know what to say. I hear
folks trying to disprove your power or your love
or even your existence, and I know there's something missing in their arguments, but I can't say
what. Still, I am not ashamed, because I know
you. I have put my trust in you, and no fancy
argument is going to change that. I may not know
everything about you, but you are a reality in my
life. Thank you.*

Unless I first believe,
I shall not understand.

—ANSELM

❈ ❈ ❈

I believe that I shall see the goodness
of the Lord in the land of the living.
Wait for the Lord; be strong, and
let your heart take courage; wait for
the Lord!

PSALM 27:13–14

❈ ❈ ❈

It only makes sense that the God of eternity
doesn't accommodate our timetables.

❈ ❈ ❈

I've been waiting, Lord, waiting for things to get better. I have trusted you with my life, trying to do the things that honor you. But when will that start to pay off? Will I have to wait for heaven to get my reward? "Be strong," you say, "and take courage." I'll try to do that. I'll keep waiting, Lord. I do believe I'll "see your goodness"—and maybe I already see it in little ways. There's a kind of calm I have in tough situations. Is that from you? I find myself empathizing with others who are going through hard times. Is compassion something you give me? I'm certainly learning to be patient with others, because I have to be patient with you. I'm waiting, Lord. Please, keep showing me your goodness.

※ ※ ※

Thomas answered him, "My Lord and my God!" Jesus said to him, "Have you believed because you have seen me? Blessed are those who have not seen and yet have come to believe."

JOHN 20:28–29

✳ ✳ ✳

Thank you, Lord Jesus, for the Apostle Thomas, who doubted your resurrection. If it weren't for him, we might assume that your resurrection was a matter of group hypnosis and that the disciples fell prey to their own wishful thinking. Your appearance in that upper room could have been just a figment of their collective imaginations— if it weren't for that skeptic who missed the first meeting. Because Thomas insisted on seeing—and touching—your wounds, we know that you stood in that room in your once-crucified, eternally resurrected body. He witnessed this and believed, and we are blessed to believe his stirring testimony. With Thomas, we boldly exclaim, "My Lord and my God!"

❈ ❈ ❈

It's a shame that Thomas will always
be known as a doubter. Asking the tough
questions, he withheld judgment for *one week*
of an otherwise faith-filled life.

❈ ❈ ❈

The hour is coming, and is now here,
when the true worshipers will worship
the Father in spirit and truth, for
the Father seeks such as these to
worship him.

JOHN 4:23

❈ ❈ ❈

O God,

I'm tired of going through the motions. Yes, I've been faithfully practicing religion for some time, but there has to be more than this. I've attended more services than I can count. I have prayed the prayers and read the verses, and I've even done some good deeds. Then why do I feel so empty? For a while I thought that I wasn't doing these things enough, that if I tried harder, I would make something happen. But then I began to realize something completely different. Maybe it was your voice calling to me; I don't know. I began to see that it wasn't about those things. It was simply about you and me. I had to stop pretending to be someone I wasn't. I just had to open my spirit to you. So, Lord, here I am.

❈ ❈ ❈

My words fly up,
my thoughts remain below.
Words without thoughts
never to heaven go.

—WILLIAM SHAKESPEARE,
HAMLET

❊ ❊ ❊

Now faith is the assurance of things
hoped for, the conviction of things
not seen.

HEBREWS 11:1

❊ ❊ ❊

Without faith it is impossible to please
God, for whoever would approach him
must believe that he exists and that he
rewards those who seek him.

HEBREWS 11:6

❊ ❊ ❊

Science is about seeing, testing, and observing. I'm having some trouble, Lord, balancing my faith with my scientific mind-set. Sometimes it seems that you're asking me to put my brain on hold, just to believe something that makes no sense. But you made my brain, right? Why give me the power to think if I'm not supposed to use it? Maybe you don't want me to turn off my brain but to go beyond it and accept what I see. But then I realize there's a great deal that I don't see, and I am certain that you are active even when I don't see you.

❋ ❋ ❋

Faith is believing what one cannot see,
and the reward of faith is to see
what one believes.

—AUGUSTINE

❋ ❋ ❋

My Lord,

I seek you. Every day I look for your presence. Some days you are as real to me as my breakfast cereal. I bounce through the hours with a confidence that you are beside me, managing every stoplight and sending every raindrop. Thank you for those days. But then there are other days, when I long to know that you are with me, but you seem strangely silent. I'm not sure what's going on there, but I press through those days, hoping that you'll break through the fog and greet me once again.

❦ ❦ ❦

If miracles happened all the time,
they wouldn't be miracles.

❦ ❦ ❦

Three times I appealed to the Lord
about this [thorn in the flesh],
that it would leave me, but he said to
me, "My grace is sufficient for you."

2 CORINTHIANS 12:8–9

❋❋ ❋❋ ❋❋

I find that the doing of the will of God leaves
me no time for disputing about his plans.

—GEORGE MACDONALD

❋❋ ❋❋ ❋❋

Lord God,
I've been praying and praying for something,
and you haven't responded. I don't understand
why you're not granting this request, because it
seems so right. It's not overly selfish. I think it
would really bring you glory if you did this for
me. But still . . . no answer. You told Paul that
your grace was sufficient. Maybe I'd better try
to figure out what that means.

❈ ❈ ❈

Truly God is good to the upright,
    to those who are pure in heart.
But as for me, my feet had almost
        stumbled;
    my steps had nearly slipped.
For I was envious of the arrogant;
    I saw the prosperity of the wicked.

PSALM 73:1–3

My Lord,

Sometimes I get the feeling that everyone else knows something I don't. Other believers seem so happy when they talk about you, as if everything is just fine in this world. But I can't help thinking about how wrong it is that the arrogant and the wicked live such carefree lives while I'm struggling. I can't go to the supermarket without seeing their pictures in magazines—our stars of entertainment and business. They act as if you don't exist, while I work hard every day to please you. And who's raking in the dough? Them, not me. Who's taking island vacations? Them, not me. Where is the justice in that? I try to be upright and pure in heart, but what's the use? Maybe there's something here that I'm missing. Please show me, dear Lord.

※ ※ ※

The psalmists often complained
about the sinful rich,
but usually something
changed their perspective.
When they came before God,
they realized that
the wealth of the wicked has
an expiration date,
while their own blessings are eternal.

※ ※ ※

Count up the questions in Scripture.
There are hundreds of them,
maybe thousands. Apparently God loves to
interact with inquisitive people.

※ ※ ※

As I went through the city and looked carefully at the objects of your worship, I found . . . an altar with the inscription "To an unknown god." What therefore you worship as unknown, this I proclaim to you.

ACTS 17:23

❋ ❋ ❋

O unknown God, I'm not sure how else to address you. I guess I've reached the point where I'm questioning everything I thought I knew. I've taken a scalpel to all the trappings of religious observance, and I'm starting fresh. There's too much hypocrisy and too many broken promises. I'm not interested in being anything other than true. So here I am, my altar stripped bare, and I have come to the sobering conclusion that I was made to worship. My knees bend in that direction. My heart cries out for my Creator. Even if I doubt everything else, I know that I must honor the One beyond me. So I come in meager faith before you, my unknown God.

Everyone who calls on the name of
the Lord shall be saved.

ROMANS 10:13

If it seems to tarry, wait for it;
>   it will surely come, it will not delay.
Look at the proud!
>   Their spirit is not right in them,
>   but the righteous live by their faith.

HABAKKUK 2:3–4

❋ ❋ ❋

Thank you, heavenly Father, for your promises.
I trust that you will honor them in due time.
O, it's no fun waiting. But I believe that you
know what timing is best, and you have all the
time in the world, and then some. Thank you,
Lord, for the peaceful spirit you provide. Yes,
I sometimes envy the arrogant, but I see the hole
in their hearts. Thank you for the abundant life
you provide me through faith.

❋ ❋ ❋

"The righteous live by faith" is a powerful maxim borrowed from Habakkuk by Paul and later Martin Luther. The original Hebrew is elegantly simple: *righteous-live-faith.* These three qualities coexist in a believer.

❊ ❊ ❊

The Lord is in his holy temple;
   let all the earth keep silence
   before him!

HABAKKUK 2:20

❊ ❊ ❊

Though the fig tree does not
   blossom...
yet I will rejoice in the Lord...
he makes my feet like the feet of a deer,
and makes me tread upon the heights.

HABAKKUK 3:17–19

While life's dark maze I tread,
and griefs around me spread, be thou my guide;
Bid darkness turn to day, wipe sorrow's tears
away, nor let me ever stray from thee aside.

—Ray Palmer,
"My Faith Looks Up to Thee"

※ ※ ※

Help me, dear Lord!
I have tried to figure things out, and I can't.
I have tried to plan out my own life, and I
haven't done so well. I have tried to answer all
the questions, explain all the mysteries, and solve
all the equations, but I have come to the end of
myself. My faith has been questioned to death.
I don't get you, and I'm not sure I ever will.
So I'm back to basics, calling for your help. I
need you in my life, Lord, and I can't make that
happen on my own. But I believe you can. In
Jesus' name, I pray. Amen.

CHAPTER 14

WHEN YOU'RE WANTING TO EXPRESS LOVE TO GOD

❊ ❊ ❊

Glory to God,
and praise, and love
be ever, ever given
by saints below and saints above,
The church in earth and heaven.

—CHARLES WESLEY,
"OH, FOR A THOUSAND TONGUES"

Hear, O Israel: The Lord is our God, the Lord alone. You shall love the Lord your God with all your heart, and with all your soul, and with all your might.

DEUTERONOMY 6:4–5

※ ※ ※

O, God of heaven and earth!
You are both the source of and the best object
of my love. Your command to me to love you is
a wonderful one, and I willingly say yes to it
with a heart full of gladness today. Please grant
that I may always love you and that I might
learn to love you wholeheartedly. You're more
than worthy of all my devotion.

※ ※ ※

They do not love that do not show their love.

—SHAKESPEARE,
THE TWO GENTLEMEN OF VERONA

O Happy race of men,
if love, which rules heaven,
rule your minds.

—BOETHIUS,
CONSOLATIONS OF PHILOSOPHY

✵ ✵ ✵

Love the Lord, all his saints!
The Lord preserves the faithful.

PSALM 31:23 (NIV)

✵ ✵ ✵

Dear Lord Jesus,
I know you've been with me throughout my
life—even before I knew you, you were there,
leading me to your side, helping me learn that
I can entrust my life to you. Now, as one who
longs to show my adoration, please guide me
into true expressions of love for you, through
praise and prayer, service and submission, faith
and obedience. Let my entire being demonstrate
the reality of the love you have established in
my heart.

I love the Lord, because he has heard
my voice and my supplications.

PSALM 116:1

Love peers intently through
the window of words to discover
the heart's true affection.

❈ ❈ ❈

*You know how I long to be heard and understood,
heavenly Father. No one has ever listened to me
as you do; no one has ever perceived who I am the
way you have. Your attentiveness to my prayers
and to the cries of my heart endear you to me
over and over again. Even when I'm not sure
what to pray, you know what it is I am longing
for (or when I ask you for things I think would
be best, you know what really is best for me).
Each time I pray, you hear my heart's cry, and
my love for you deepens that much more.*

❈ ❈ ❈

Let all who take refuge in you rejoice;
    let them ever sing for joy.
Spread your protection over them,
    so that those who love your name
      may exult in you.

PSALM 5:11

❋ ❋ ❋

You are the protector of my soul and my life! I feel safe knowing you are keeping watch over me day and night. You never sleep. You never tire. You are always vigilant. I long to tell you at this moment how much I love you and how much your protective love means to me. There is no safeguard on earth to which I can run and be kept perfectly safe as I can with you.

❋ ❋ ❋

Under His wings—oh,
what precious enjoyment!
There will I hide till life's trials are o'er;
Sheltered, protected, no evil can harm me;
Resting in Jesus I'm safe evermore.

—William O. Cushing,
"Under His Wings"

❋ ❋ ❋

I trusted in your steadfast love;
my heart shall rejoice in your salvation.

Psalm 13:5

❋ ❋ ❋

In your unfailing love, Lord Jesus, you have provided salvation for me. Your sacrifice moves me each time I consider it. Only you have loved me—only you could love me—in this way. Your love has planted the seed of love in my heart that continues to grow. I will never forget the day you showed me your salvation, and I will never stop rejoicing in it. Eternity itself cannot wear out my heart of grateful love for you.

※ ※ ※

If ever we doubt God's love for us
or if ever our love for him grows faint,
we need only recall the Cross.

※ ※ ※

If the devil tries to harass you today,
remind him who your heavenly Father is.

※ ※ ※

I love you, O Lord, my strength....
I call upon the Lord, who is worthy
to be praised, so I shall be saved from
my enemies.

PSALM 18:1, 3

※ ※ ※

Dear God,
I enjoy being able to freely express my love for you
in houses of worship and among other Christians.
Thank you, Lord, for the church, where I can
praise you and worship you with an open and
sincere heart. Let my worship be pleasing to
you, not a show for others or a rote exercise of
tradition, but a living sacrifice of love to you,
holy and acceptable in your sight.

※ ※ ※

I know sometimes my enemies seem like the people in my life who push against me, who harm me, or who don't care about me. But help me remember today that my true and most formidable enemy is not made of flesh and blood. The enemy of my soul is the one who seeks to steal my joy, destroy my faith, and kill my hope. But praise you, Lord! You have conquered him! You have defeated him and rendered his schemes futile when they are used against me. There is no enemy—no power or principality—that can change my standing with you. I love you, and I love belonging to you, almighty Father.

※ ※ ※

O Lord, I love the house in which
you dwell, and the place where your
glory abides.... My foot stands on level
ground; in the great congregation I will
bless the Lord.

PSALM 26:8, 12

❋ ❋ ❋

When I gather with God's people,
the fellowship helps me forget myself.
When I praise with God's people,
the worship helps me remember my Lord.

❋ ❋ ❋

Your steadfast love, O Lord,
extends to the heavens,
your faithfulness to the clouds.... How
precious is your steadfast love,
O God!

PSALM 36:5, 7

It doesn't matter how foolish or fearful or stubborn or selfish I've been, Lord. When I come to you with the sorrow of sin in my heart, your faithfulness and your love never reject me; you always take me in. Everything you do, you do faithfully: love, provide, protect, teach, lead, guide, help, discipline, forgive, save, restore, redeem . . . the list could go on and on. How good you are to me! I love your faithfulness. I love you. Keep me in your steadfast love forever, my faithful Lord.

❈ ❈ ❈

Faithfulness is perhaps the quality
most easily taken for granted and yet
the most lamented when lacking.

❈ ❈ ❈

May all who seek you rejoice and
be glad in you; may those who love
your salvation say continually,
"Great is the Lord!"

PSALM 40:16

※ ※ ※

*I feel kind of giddy sometimes when I think
about the fact that you, the God of the universe,
love me; that you, the one who called forth the
wonders of earth and sky, know me by name and
care for me. What thoughts! You bowl me over
with fresh revelations of your saving love, and
I'm glad all over again.*

※ ※ ※

Love is, above all, the gift of oneself.

—JEAN ANOUILH, *ARDÈLE*

※ ※ ※

By day the Lord commands
his steadfast love, and at night
his song is with me, a prayer to
the God of my life.

Psalm 42:8

❈ ❈ ❈

O Lord, my God!
When I in awesome wonder
Consider all the worlds Thy hands have made,
I see the stars,
I hear the rolling thunder,
Thy power throughout the universe displayed,
Then sings my soul, my Saviour God, to Thee,
How great Thou art, how great Thou art!

—Stuart K. Hine,
"How Great Thou Art"

There isn't a time, day or night, when I am not aware of your presence with me. My very heartbeat reminds me that you sustain my life. Every meal reminds me that you care for my needs. The roof over my head on a stormy night reminds me that you shelter me in your goodness. All of your work bears the hallmarks of abiding love. How can I not sing of it, pray in gratitude for it, and love you back for it? How blessed I am at all times by all the ways you demonstrate your love in my life!

※ ※ ※

Birds must wait for the dawn's arrival to begin their praises, but my song knows no such constraint, for the Son of Love is ever brightening the horizon of my soul.

※ ※ ※

The Lord is my shepherd; I have all that I need.... Surely your goodness and unfailing love will pursue me all the days of my life.

Psalm 23:1, 6 (NLT)

※ ※ ※

Sometimes I get so wrapped up with tending to the stuff of life that I forget to stop and enjoy the fact that you are taking care of me, that you are right here with me, and that your goodness and unfailing love never leave me. Your presence with me is my greatest need, and that need is met every moment of every day; I don't need to chase after it, earn it, go to the store to buy it, repair it, or replace it. I want to stop right now and just relish the blessing of being in your care, dear Shepherd of my life. I love you and want to follow you forever.

※ ※ ※

The King of love my shepherd is,
Whose goodness faileth never;
I nothing lack if I am His
And He is mine forever.

—HENRY W. BAKER,
"THE KING OF LOVE MY SHEPHERD IS"

We love him,
because he first loved us.

1 John 4:19 (KJV)

※ ※ ※

It's your love for me, dear Lord, that has inspired and initiated my love for you. I think I would have been afraid of you or indifferent toward you if you hadn't shown your love to me. Thank you for reaching out to me and opening your heart to me and for showing me how to open my heart to you. And even as you are the one who has begun this relationship, I pray that you will also keep it and cause it to grow throughout my life until this fragile love of mine is made complete when I finally meet you face to face. How I look forward to that day!

※ ※ ※

Because your steadfast love is better
than life, my lips will praise you.
So I will bless you as long as I live.

PSALM 63:3–4

There is no harvest for the heart alone;
The seed of love must be
Eternally
Resown.

—ANNE MORROW LINDBERGH,
"SECOND SOWING"

The heart satisfied by God's love becomes
a haven to the world around it.

※ ※ ※

What would my life be without your love,
heavenly Father? I can only imagine: empty,
selfish, cold, dark. My life might have all the
trappings of success, but it would be an utter
failure. How glad I am to know your faithful
love: to wake up in it, work in it, play in it, lie
down to sleep in it! I count myself privileged in
this life, no matter my circumstances, as long as
I know your love and can love you in return.
There is no enjoyment more exquisite than
sensing your love surrounding me and holding
me close to your heart.

✻ ✻ ✻

I will sing of your steadfast love,
O Lord, forever; with my mouth
I will proclaim your faithfulness
to all generations.

PSALM 89:1

Sometimes there seems to be an unspoken rule that faith is a private personal matter to be kept to oneself. But, Lord, how can I keep the wonders of your love all to myself? I have children and grandchildren whom I want to tell about you and your unfailing love. Please grant me your sensitivity to their needs and to the right timing for spiritual conversations. I need your Spirit of wisdom to know how and when to talk to them about your faithfulness and love. I so want them to enjoy the benefits of knowing you, as I have been privileged to do. Let your own love spill over from my life into theirs so that the next generations may be blessed by you as well.

※ ※ ※

Satisfy us in the morning with your
steadfast love, so that we may rejoice
and be glad all our days.

PSALM 90:14

❋ ❋ ❋

*Your love comes to me each morning, dear Lord.
I feel it. I wake up in it. But sometimes I push
it aside to tackle the "chores" of the day. O, help
me stop and linger in it more often, to soak it in
and be refreshed by it. I know that when I do
that, the day's duties take their rightful place.
Relationships are given priority. Love flows from
you like a river, carrying me along and washing
over me and making fresh everything I do and
every relationship I form. How I love your
steadfast love! Let it be the crowning glory of each
new day, the blessing of each human encounter.*

❋ ❋ ❋

Although you have not seen him,
you love him; and even though you
do not see him now, you believe in him
and rejoice with an indescribable and
glorious joy.

1 PETER 1:8

❋ ❋ ❋

Fairest Lord Jesus,
Ruler of all nature,
O Thou of God and man the Son;
Thee will I cherish,
Thee will I honor,
Thou my soul's glory, joy, and crown.

—MÜNSTER GESANGBUCH,
"FAIREST LORD JESUS"

❋ ❋ ❋

I live in the hope of seeing you one day, dear Lord Jesus. You are the one whose love has saved me and in whose love I am sustained. I have not seen you yet, but I have known the reality of your love better than I have known any "seen" or tangible thing on this earth. My love waits for you, and it does not grow weary, because it grows up out of the seed of your own unfailing love. In your precious name, I pray. Amen.

ACKNOWLEDGMENTS

PHOTO CREDITS